A colour guide to familiar

BUTTERFLIES

llars and Chrysalides

A colour guide to familiar
BUTTERFLIES
Caterpillars
and Chrysalides

By Josef Moucha
Illustrated by Bohumil Vančura

Special consultant Dr. Ivo Novák
Translated by Dr. Ivan Pokorný
Graphic design: Soňa Valoušková

This paperback edition published 1983 by
OCTOPUS BOOKS LIMITED
59 Grosvenor Street, London W 1

ISBN 0 7064 1975 8

Printed in Czechoslovakia
3/10/05/51-09

CONTENTS

Foreword   7

**Origin of Butterflies and Their Classification
in the Animal Kingdom**   9
    Historical Development of Butterflies   9
    Classification of Butterflies in the Animal Kingdom   9
    Names of Butterflies   11

**The Life of Butterflies and Development
of Individual Stages**   13
    Laying and Development of Eggs   14
    Life of the Caterpillar   14
    The Chrysalis Stage   16
    The Adult Butterfly   17

Body Structure of Different Stages of Development   19
    The Adult   19
    The Egg   21
    The Caterpillar   22
    The Chrysalis   24

The Variability of Butterflies   26
    Individual Variability   26
    Sexual Dimorphism   27
    Seasonal Variability   27
    Geographical Variability   28

Distribution of Butterflies   29
    Vertical Distribution   29
    Horizontal Distribution   30
    Number of Butterfly Species   32

Significance of Butterflies and Moths in Nature   33
    Useful Species   33
    Pests   33
    Indifferent Species   34

Enemies and Diseases of Butterflies   35
    Virus Diseases   35
    Bacterial Diseases and Microsporidia   35
    Fungal Diseases   36
    Predators and Other Enemies   36
    Defence of Butterflies Against Their Enemies   38

Plates   39—167

Catching of Butterflies, Caterpillars and Pupae   169
    Hunting Methods   170
    Collecting and Breeding of Caterpillars   172
    Collecting and Breeding of Pupae   174
    Pinning of Butterflies   175
    Setting Boards and Other Apparatus   176
    Setting of Wings   178
    Data Labels   179
    Preparation of Caterpillars   180
    Starting a Collection   180

Bibliography   183

Index of Common Names   186

Index of Latin Names   189

FOREWORD

The originally vast profusion of natural species is gradually diminishing, many members of the European fauna having become extinct, and others existing now only in reservations and zoological gardens. Impenetrable primeval forests have disappeared and most of the big beasts of prey and other large wild animals have vanished. However, we are left with a diverse and multicoloured mosaic of flowers and birds and an immense number of small and large insects. What an orchid is among flowers and a bird of paradise among birds, the lovely butterfly is among insects. While the exotic wonders of nature are inaccessible to most of us, the butterflies and moths occur in tens of thousands of species and billions of specimens all over the world. Scientists have described and named over a hundred thousand species of butterflies and moths, and estimate that every tenth species in the world belongs to the large order of *Lepidoptera*. These insects appear almost everywhere. They are found in the mountains, in deep valleys and forests, in meadows and fields, on the steppes and even in deserts. Lepidopterous insects are not only pretty and varied but also have an extremely interesting life cycle. The transformation during different stages of development has always attracted the attention of philosophers and observers of nature. The deeper the mystery of these processes is studied the more it must be admired. For this reason the caterpillars and pupae, as well as the butterflies, are described in this book. Those selected enable the reader to see the most beautiful and agriculturally important species in addition to those deserving protection because of their rarity. The painter has tried to picture butterflies as we see them in nature — resting or on the wing. The caterpillars, too, are portrayed on their foodplants, as found in nature.

Many a reader may wish to start a collection of *Lepidoptera*. He will perhaps welcome advice on the way they should be caught, bred, and prepared for a collection. Collecting these lovely insects rewards every collector with entertainment, joy, and the satisfaction of preserving their ephemeral beauty for the future. Many collectors advance from simple collecting to purposeful effort to gain detailed knowledge of the butterflies and moths and the environment in which they live. This may result in valuable contributions to the understanding of the fauna of an area.

Although the species described in this book are basically European, many of them occur in the Americas and the Orient as described in the plate captions; and the introductory chapter on classification is common to all species everywhere.

The first part of this book contains general information about the life of butterflies; the second part presents a selection of species with short descriptions of the butterflies themselves, their occurrence and distribution, life cycle, foodplants, etc. The book is intended to give only a general guidance. In Denmark or the Netherlands the individual species occur at different times of the year and have a different number of generations than in central or southern Europe. The book is not a textbook of *Lepidoptera* (study of butterflies and moths) but it attempts to give a concise summary of our knowledge of the life of many interesting butterflies.

ORIGIN OF BUTTERFLIES
AND THEIR CLASSIFICATION
IN THE ANIMAL KINGDOM

Historical Development of Butterflies

Butterflies and moths *(Lepidoptera)* are a separate order of the class of insects *(Insecta)*. From the point of view of historical development the *Ledidoptera* are a relatively young group and the butterflies are among the youngest. Very little paleontological evidence is available to help us to estimate the approximate age of this order. When trying to make such an estimate it is often taken into account that the existence of *Lepidoptera* is usually associated with that of the flowering plants which first occured at the end of the Mesozoic period. Remnants of the flowering plants from this era have been found. The remote ancestors of the *Lepidoptera* and their most primitive species probably lived even earlier, perhaps as early as the Carboniferous period.

The known remnants of lepidopterous insects come from the beginning of the Tertiary period. At that time there was already a great number of species, not differing significantly from those of the present day, and it seems that the proper phylogenetical development must have taken place hundreds of millions of years earlier.

The contemporary stage of development can be visualized as a cross section of the final phase of the long developmental chain involving not only *Lepidoptera* but, at the same time, the whole of the animal kingdom and it is characterized by an abundance of species developing from common ancestors.

Classification of Butterflies in the Animal Kingdom

To be able to comprehend the vast quantity of existing species the scientists have devised an extensive and methodically arranged classification system. They placed all the known species of animals in distinct systematic groups trying to observe the succession of organisms from the simplest to more complicated, and from the phylogenetically older forms to the younger ones, showing the interrelationships that have formed during the phylogenetic development.

This classification makes it possible to identify single species by means of certain features and place them in the system. *Lepidoptera* may be classified according to the following simplified scheme:

1. Kingdom	Animals *(Animalia)*
2. Phylum	Arthropods *(Arthropoda)*
3. Class	Insects *(Insecta)*
4. Order	Butterflies and moths *(Lepidoptera)*

These "higher" systematic categories determine unequivocally the location of butterflies in the animal kingdom.

Precise classification and nomenclature of the groups formed in this way goes further; order is divided into suborders, superfamily into families, genera, and finally species and subspecies.

Most collectors are not very interested in the classification of butterflies in relation to the animal kingdom. Their interest is more often confined to the order and "lower" subunits of the classification. The "mysterious" terms are best understood from an example. Simplified classification of the Large Copper is as follows:

4. Order:	Butterflies and moths *(Lepidoptera)*
5. Sub-order:	Frenates *(Frenata)*
6. Family:	Lycaenids *(Lycaenidae)*
7. Sub-family:	Lycaenines *(Lycaeninae)*
8. Genus:	The Copper *(Lycaena* Fabricius, 1807*)*
9. Species:	The Large Copper *(Lycaena dispar* Haworth, 1803)
10. Sub-species:	*Lycaena dispar dispar* Haworth, 1803 *Lycaena dispar batava* Oberthur, 1920 *Lycaena dispar rutila* Werneburg, 1864 etc.

Names of Butterflies

Every species has two names, every subspecies three. The first is the name of the genus, the second is the name of the species, and the third of the subspecies (used for more detailed classification). In addition, the name of the author who first described the species comes after the name of the species or subspecies. In modern literature the year of the first species description is appended to the name of the author. In our case it was A. H. Haworth, the author of the "Lepidoptera Britannica", published in London in 1803—29. The form according to which the species was described is called the nominate form.

The original name of the species and subspecies is binding. In the case of discovery of a name older than the one in common use the latter must be replaced by the former. The names having become invalid in this way are called synonyms. The rule of priority is strictly observed as the accurate naming system could not be maintained otherwise. At present a comparatively large number of changes in the names of butterflies are still made as new facts are being found on the basis of the study of old collections and literature, but it is to be hoped that the species terminology will soon become established so that a change of name will become necessary only in exceptional cases, if at all.

Deriving the names of genera is more complicated, although, in principle, the same. The genus is, to a large extent, an artificial category; it reflects the personal opinion of the scientist and his "school", particularly in the interpretation of the relationships of different species. Further changes of the nomenclature of genera can be expected when further progress is made in the study of morphology, anatomy and genetics.

The rule of priority does not apply to the units lower than subspecies, i.e. names of individual or seasonal forms, hybrids, etc. These names are formed freely and their being respected is a question of custom. The name of a genus is easy to recognize because it is always written with a capital letter. Conversely, the name of the species or subspecies is written with a small initial letter even when derived from the name of a person, e.g. the White *Pieris mannii* Mayer, 1851. One peculiarity can be shown in the above-mentioned example; only the original name in its full extent is acknowledged despite the error in grammar which has crept in. This White butterfly was named after the collector Josef Mann (1804—1889) who worked as a painter, collector, and preparator in the Collection Room of the Viennese court. Although the correct form of the name would be *Pieris manni* we are obliged to conform to the convention and use the original *Pieris mannii* thus perpetuating the grammatical error!

The national names of butterflies became universally accepted only in the case of agriculturally important or injurious species. In the case of less well known butterflies national names have not achieved universal acceptance and sometimes do not even exist. In most languages the current national names of butterflies do not correspond to the zoological system. The binominal terminology, similar to Latin, has developed in some languages, e.g. Czech or Polish. Most collectors eventually become familiar with the Latin nomenclature of butterflies which simplifies international communication.

The scientific terminology used in this book is in agreement with the classification of European species in the handbook "A Field Guide to the Butterflies of Britain and Europe" by L. H. Higgins and N. D. Riley, published in London in 1970.

THE LIFE OF BUTTERFLIES
AND DEVELOPMENT OF INDIVIDUAL STAGES

Metamorphosis is an extraordinary phenomenon observed in the world of insects. Apart from a small number of primitive forms, all insects undergo a complicated change. With the exception of the originally wingless insects (e.g. *Collembola* and *Diplura*) the newly hatched individual differs in appearance from its parents. The simpler, developmentally older types grow wings, ovipositors and other adult characteristics gradually in the course of their development and the pupa (or resting) stage does not occur in these forms. This kind of development is called incomplete metamorphosis or heterometabolia because the basic structure of the body is retained and the organs mentioned develop gradually during growth.

Butterflies belong to the other, developmentally higher and younger group with complete metamorphosis or holometabolia. The egg hatches and a small caterpillar of limited mobility crawls out of the shell. It spends most of its life on a leaf of the foodplant, preoccupied mainly with feeding. Its long cylinder-shaped body and the head, equipped with rather inefficient sensory organs, bear hardly any resemblance to the winged, beautifully shaped and coloured adult it will eventually become.

This remarkable change takes place in the inactive pupa stage. All tissues inside the hard pupal covering are dissolved to an amorphous matter and an entirely new and changed living being begins to form. After a period of development, which may last for several days or months to as long as several years depending on the species, the imago (adult butterfly) leaves the pupa.

Laying and Development of Eggs

The female butterfly usually lays eggs directly onto the food-plant of the caterpillar. Sometimes, however, they may be dropped at random in a place where the foodplants grow and can easily be reached.

The number of eggs varies from several dozens to hundreds and even thousands in the case of some of the moths. The females lay eggs singly or in groups, occasionally arranging them in small heaps. For example, the Small Tortoiseshell or the Peacock Butterfly lay a batch of eggs on the leaf of a stinging nettle in the spring. The caterpillars, staying close together, feed on the leaves, often stripping the plant completely. The Large White, which lays batches of yellow eggs, stuck to the leaves of cabbage, kohlrabi, and other cruciferous plants, arranges them neatly side by side. Freshly laid butterfly eggs are usually yellowish-white, yellow-orange, grey, or greenish; later, particularly shortly before hatching, they turn dark.

Life of the Caterpillar

Having hatched, the caterpillar devours a part or the whole of the egg shell and after a short lapse of time starts to feed on the foodplant. The development of the caterpillar is divided into several (mostly five or six) clear-cut stages or instars. After a certain period of time the growth of the caterpillar is arrested for a few days and moulting takes place. The length of this period is influenced by temperature or the time of year; in some species it takes several days but may take as long as weeks or even months. At the time of moulting the caterpillar does not feed, it attaches itself to a leaf, twig, a piece of bark or a stone and strips off the old skin, very much as snakes do. This stage is very critical for the caterpillar because its body is soft, vulnerable and defenceless.

The caterpillar's shape, colour, size, and way of life varies tremendously. Caterpillars are, in many ways, adapted to their environment. On the one hand this adaptation is linked with their feeding habits, such as on leaves, inside leaves, roots, stalks, or flowers, and on the other hand it provides a defence against enemies through protective or deterrent colouring, hairs, bristles, spikes, etc. Such adaptation is especially characteristic of the moths, but is known in a number of butterflies, too.

The caterpillars of many butterflies, e.g. the Swallowtail, the Poplar Admiral, the Blues, etc. are solitary, as opposed to others living in large groups like the Peacock Butterfly, Camberwell Beauty, etc. Some aggregations of moth caterpillars like the Tussock Moths, Brown-tails and the Beautiful Mining Moths, make large and heavy nests consisting of leaves and twigs spun together with silk. The butterflies rarely form nests; one of the few examples of a nest-making butterfly is the Black-veined White. The nests protect the caterpillars against adverse temperature and enemies. If the butterfly does not hibernate in the form of a pupa or as an adult (or imago) the caterpillar makes a hiding place in a folded leaf onto which it grips by means of a pad of spun silk. Alternatively, some caterpillars hibernate in the open, attached to twigs or leaves. The Poplar Admiral is an example of the former mode of hibernation, the Alpine Clouded Yellow of the latter.

Caterpillars of some species of the Blues spend a part of their life in ant-hills where they are looked after by the ants (e.g. *M. arion* L.). Such caterpillars are specially adapted for this care and sometimes are entirely dependent on it.

So called monophagous species of caterpillars are able to feed on only one kind of foodplant, e.g. the caterpillars of the Moorland Clouded Yellow on bog whortleberry, or the caterpillars of the Small Blue on kidney vetch.

In contrast the oligophagous caterpillars can feed on several plants of a certain family, e.g. the Swallowtail on a variety of umbelliferous plants. The least specialized, the polyphagous caterpillars, feed on many species of plants. Few butterflies fall into this category (e.g. the Painted Lady, the Black-veined White), the majority of species being oligophagous.

The choice of a particular part of a foodplant is characteristic, too. Most caterpillars feed on leaves, either starting from the edge or eating round holes in them. Small caterpillars devour only the superficial layers of leaves, upperside or underside, leaving transparent windows of the intact epidermis. Certain species like the Black-veined White prefer the buds and cause considerable damage to the fruit trees.

The development of the caterpillar may take anything from several days to a year or more, especially in high mountains or polar regions. For example, the development of some Satyrids is very slow; so the number of generations of a species in a year depends on the length of its development.

The Chrysalis Stage

Chrysalis or pupa is the inactive stage in the development of butterflies and moths. The front part of the chrysalis with the head, antennae, wings and legs is immobile, any degree of mobility being limited to the abdominal segments. The pupa has no defences against unfavourable effects of environment. A pupa cannot escape heat, diseases or predators, and if it is to survive, the caterpillar, before pupating, must take adequate precautions to counter dangers threatening the future pupa. For this reason instinct drives caterpillars to be very careful when looking for a place to pupate. They frequently crawl long distances to find suitable places where they bury themselves underground, nibble out hiding cells, spin cocoons or fold leaves. The pupae of the butterflies are seldom enclosed in cocoons but are attached to twigs or leaves by a spun pad or silk girdle.

The duration of the pupal stage varies in different species. In summer the imago usually emerges in one or two weeks, except for the species with only one generation in a year; but if winter intervenes it takes several months before the butterfly can emerge from the hard pupal covering. It is not uncommon for pupae of some moths to persist for two years before the adult insect hatches.

The Adult Butterfly

The newly emerged imago does not resemble very much the adult butterfly flying from flower to flower. It is soft, has only small limp wings and is at first incapable of flight. The wings grow to their full size within ten to twenty minutes but even then they are very soft and it may take up to two hours before the butterfly is able to fly safely.

Like the caterpillar, the imago is a mobile stage in the life of the butterfly and it is perhaps not surprising that it is more eventful than that of the caterpillar. Producing offspring — the next generation — is the main task of the adult butterfly and everything is directly or indirectly channelled to this objective. After the male has fertilized the female and she has laid eggs, they have both fulfilled their role in nature and die. All butterflies do not have the same length of life and it may take a long time before some of them achieve their reproductive goal.

Some species of *Lepidoptera* have an underdeveloped proboscis (or tongue) and do not feed, e.g. Tussock-Moths, Tiger-Moths and some of the Hawk Moths. They live on the fat deposits accumulated during the caterpillars' life and die after some days. The butterflies and moths which suck nectar live several weeks or months and can even hibernate through the winter.

In certain species of butterflies the interesting phenomenon of migration appears. Moths migrate too, but migration was first observed in the butterflies as they fly during the day. The most famous traveller among butterflies is undoubtedly the Monarch, an American species with the Latin name *Danaus plexippus* L., which can fly thousands of miles north and then back south every year. The trees in which these butterflies hibernate, clustered by thousands, are protected by law as a natural curiosity. Similar travellers are found among the European species. For example, the Painted Lady does not hibernate in central Europe; it comes from the Mediterranean every spring. The Clouded Yellow, the Bath White and the Red Admiral migrate from the south to central and northern Europe to settle

17

in this region for the summer. In contrast to this, the Large White migrates within the range of its normal distribution area, either farther north or to a different region in the temperate zone. Migration is usually linked with the reproduction process. In the area where the butterflies arrive as migrants they form a summer generation which partly dies out in autumn, and partly in all probability migrates back to the south.

BODY STRUCTURE OF DIFFERENT STAGES OF DEVELOPMENT

The Adult

The body of the adult butterfly (imago) differs entirely, in the way it is built, from its immature stages — egg, caterpillar and pupa. Like other insects, the butterfly has three separate body parts, head, thorax and abdomen.

The head bears noticeably large, most commonly hemi-spherical, compound eyes. (Fig. 1.) They are bulging, shiny, have different colours, and consist of a large quantity of tiny visual cones or ommatidia. The antennae serve as organs of smell, the palps as organs of touch. The antennae project from the top of the head-capsule and vary in shape. They may be

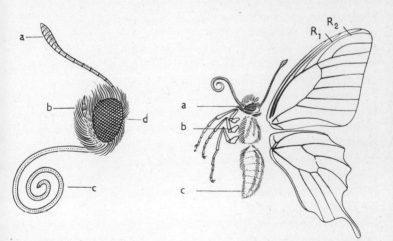

Fig. 1. Head of a butterfly: a) antenna, b) palp, c) proboscis, d) eye.

Fig. 2. Structure of the body of a butterfly: a) head, b) thorax and legs, c) abdomen.

thread-like, bristle-shaped or comb-like in the moths. The butterflies always have club-like antennae, hence the name *Rhopalocera*. Different species have a different shape and length of proboscis, which is used for sucking nectar or water. The butterflies possess a rather long proboscis coiled in a spiral; they unwind it only when sucking.

The head is attached to the thorax by a delicate short membranous neck. The thorax consists of three parts — prothorax, mesothorax and metathorax — which form a compact unit at superficial observation, but internally the sections are morphologically separated. Two pairs of membranous wings, covered with numerous fine small multiform and multicoloured scales, grow out of the thorax. Some male butterflies have scent scales, which are connected to the scent glands and emit a characteristic odour, sometimes detectable even by humans. The scent of the Small White, for instance, is well-known. These scent scales form complete patches on the forewings of the butterflies. The scales are inserted into the skin of the wings by means of small projections. Their colour is determined either by pigment or by the purely physical phenomenon of light deflection or reflection. The scales are hollow and the light reflection and deflection results in the formation of shiny and coloured patches on the wings, e.g. in the Blues, the Fritillaries, and the Purple Emperor.

The wings are reinforced by a network of veins, which have been classified and named. The number, course and arrangement of the wing veins are not the same in all butterflies and moths and distinctions in veining are a help in classification. The forewing is reinforced at the front edge by a costal and sub-costal vein. Other branched veins further back are called radial, medial, cubital and anal. Their branches are designated by number, e.g. radial R_1, R_2; medial M_1, M_2, etc. The abbreviations indicating the names of the veins are written with capital letters, while the areas outlined by the veins are designated by small letters.

There are three pairs of thin legs on the thorax, serving mainly for gripping. The forelegs of the males — and females in some cases — of some butterflies (e.g. Satyrids and Nymphalids) are rudimentary and of no use. The end of the tarsus is equipped with a two-pronged claw and a pad enabling the butterfly to hold on even to smooth surfaces.

The abdomen is cylinder-shaped, slim and fairly long in the butterflies. Originally it consisted of ten segments similar in both external and internal structure. During the historical development the last two or three segments became adapted for another function, i.e. became incorporated in the external copulatory organs, so that only seven of the original ones are externally visible in the female and eight in the male.

The copulatory organs, particularly their hard, sclerotinized parts, are very important from the point of view of the classification of butterflies and moths. They are indispensable for the determination of species whose colouring and other features bear a very close resemblance. The anatomy of the copulatory organs is very complicated and differs in every species but varies only very slightly among individual members of a species. The male and female copulatory organs of one species form a closed system, often compared to a lock with the corresponding key. Strengthened by physiological and behavioural inhibitions, this system prevents cross pairing of unrelated species. Scientists have described the parts of the copulatory organs and have given them many names. This subject is very complex and whole books have been written about it.

The Egg

The shape of the eggs is characteristic for every species. They are about 0.2 to 1 mm wide but the length or height often exceeds 1 mm, especially in the butterflies. When seen from above the eggs are usually circular, oval, kidney-shaped or roundly quadrangular. Some moths' eggs are long and slender, others short and flat. In the butterflies there are two major types of eggs (Fig. 3 A). The first type is the smooth hemispherical egg (e.g. that of the Swallowtail), the second one is the high, slender, ribbed egg, like that of the Whites and Nymphalids.

Fig. 3. The life cycle of a butterfly:
    A — egg (left — egg of the Large White, centre and right — egg of
    the Scarce Swallowtail) a) base, b) height, c) width.

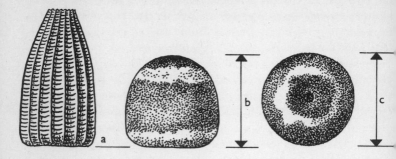

The egg is completely encased in the egg shell (chorion). There is a minute channel, called micropyle, situated either at the top or the side of the egg through which the spermatozoa reach the female germ cell in order to fertilize it. The structure of the shell round the micropyle could be likened to a rosette of leaves or a net. The micropylar zone characterizes different species of butterflies and moths and can be of help in determining the species when only eggs are found.

The rest of the egg surface exhibits a fine or, alternatively, coarse patterned structure, but may also be completely smooth. The shell may be furrowed in a net-like pattern, stippled, covered with raised dots, notched, hairy or spiked. The ground plan of the egg often resembles a cog-wheel.

The Caterpillar

The caterpillar has a long, worm-like body consisting of the head and thirteen segments. The first three segments form the thorax and each bears a pair of so called thoracic legs which are strong and simply built. The remaining ten segments constitute the abdomen. The abdominal feet arise from the third, fourth, fifth and sixth abdominal segments and the anal orifice is located between the feet of the tenth segment. These soft abdominal feet have small hooklets which assist in crawling. The caterpillars of all butterflies have legs as described above but in some moths the number of legs is smaller. The typical looping movement of the geometrid caterpillars is caused by the fact that they have abdominal feet only on the sixth and the tenth segments

The caterpillar has sizeable biting mouth parts. The important silk spinning organ opens into the mouth via the silk tube. The caterpillars of butterflies do not produce much silk but do spin some before moulting or pupating in order to get a grip on leaves or other surfaces. In contrast, the silk glands of certain moths are enormous and the silk production is immense. The Silkworm is the best-known example.

The skin of caterpillars, even those seemingly bald, is covered with many bristles and fine hairs growing either directly from the skin or from various projections. The skin itself has a delicate structure made up of spikes and bulges visible, as a rule, only under a microscope at considerable magnification. The body hairs are either sparse or dense. The bristles and hairs of caterpillars, like the copulatory organs of imagines, are very valuable from the point of view of the systematic classification of *Lepidoptera*. There is a subsidiary branch of science called chetotaxy which deals with the naming and classifying of caterpillar hairs.

Different caterpillars display innumerable shades of coloration. These range from plain green, yellow and brown to

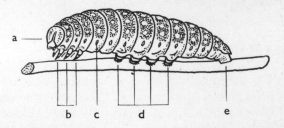
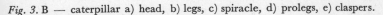

Fig. 3. B — caterpillar a) head, b) legs, c) spiracle, d) prolegs, e) claspers.

coloured stripes, dots and various bright patterns. The appearance is accentuated by the shape of the body and hairs. Many pigments go to make the final colouring of the caterpillar and during its development the colouring undergoes frequent changes.

The Chrysalis

Compared with the caterpillar or imago, the shape of the pupa or chrysalis is fairly simple. All processes take place within the hard case that reflects, to some extent only, the outlines of future organs of the imago (antennae, legs, wings, etc.). Except for the two or three families of the most primitive small *Lepidoptera*, all moths and butterflies have a type of pupa called "pupa obtecta". It is short, cylindrical or spindle-shaped; hard and almost immobile; usually bald or, rarely, covered with sparse hair.

The pupae of the butterflies either lie loose or are attached to the base by several fibres that have been produced by the caterpillar before pupating. Some pupae, like those of the Nymphalids and Satyrids, hang upside down suspended by the end of the tail, which is known as the cremaster. Others, such as Whites and Swallowtails, stand erect, supported by the cremaster and a girdle of strong silk fibre spun round the thorax. The pupae of moths often rest in cells or cocoons made of silk fibres or

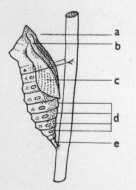

Fig. 3. C — chrysalis (pupa)
  a) head, b) sheaths of antennae,
  c) sheaths of wings,
  d) segments with spiracle,
  e) cremaster.

pieces of plants, bark, wood, grains of sand, etc. Many caterpillars of moths pupate in the earth.

The colouring of the pupae varies but is not very conspicuous. Pupae of butterflies are light green, yellowish or grey and only rarely brightly coloured. The pupa of the Large White is dotted with black. Some Nymphalid pupae are decorated with metallic patches. The pupae of moths hidden in the earth or in cocoons are mostly plain brown, red-brown, dark brown or almost black. Pupae of different species can be identified mainly by considering the overall shape and coloration of the pupa and by noting the structure of the cremaster and the different characteristic little hollows or grooves in the hard pupal shells.

THE VARIABILITY OF BUTTERFLIES

The size, design and colour of butterflies, as well as their behaviour, physiological adaptation, etc., are subject to considerable variability. This variability may be inherent, and appear either in the species as a whole or only in one of the sexes. It may also be influenced by external factors affecting individuals or whole populations.

Individual Variability

It is impossible to find two identical individuals in nature. Nevertheless, every species is characterized by certain, essentially similar main features common to all the individual members. Individual variability comprises deviations from the average or the norm, as the case may be. These deviations are pot, as a rule, hereditary and depend, to a large extent, on the external environment; changes of temperature and humidity play the most important role. The lay observer can most easily appreciate deviations in colour and design. These are so called individual forms, also known as forms (abbreviated f.) or aberrations (ab.) in older literature. Formerly collectors concentrated on looking for the specimens with deviant patterns, describing them and giving them names. Several hundred different forms of the Chalk-hill Blue have been described in England. The Apollo has achieved similar notoriety on the continent and its geographical variability has often been mistaken for an individual one. As regards systematic classification, the naming of different forms is pointless and makes already complicated nomenclature even more so. On the whole, it is more important to investigate the individual variability under set and recurring conditions and the influences causing it.

Sexual Dimorphism

Sexual dimorphism is a special type of variability. The two sexes may differ from each other only by the size or the structure of the internal and external reproductive organs. Quite often, however, the males differ from the females also in shape and colour. There are a number of examples among butterflies of this purely genetically determined variability.

The male Large White has black wing-tops, whereas the female has, in addition, also large black dots on the wings. The male of the Brimstone is lemon yellow; the female is creamy white. The male Purple Emperor exhibits beautifully changeable blue coloration; in the females it is absent. The male Blues are mostly blue, while the female are often dark brown. Some of the male Satyrids can be distinguished from the females because the former have dark patches of scent scales, laid on in thin bands, on the forewings.

Seasonal Variability

Ecologically determined seasonal variability is particularly outstanding in Europe. Without doubt the seasonal variability is caused by the environment effecting different developmental stages, especially that of the caterpillar. The length of the day during the stage of the caterpillar development, climatic effects, changes in the quality of food, etc., are among the factors that substantially influence the seasonal variability. Alternating periods of droughts and rains in the tropics also lead to formation of various seasonal forms.

Comparison between the spring and summer generations of the Map Butterfly *(Araschnia levana* L.*)* has become a textbook example of seasonal forms. The ground colour of the wings of the two forms differs markedly. It has been proved experimentally that the caterpillars living in spring, during the long day period of May and June give rise to the adult butterflies of the black summer generation (f. *prorsa* L.), while the autumn caterpillars, mature during the short day period,

27

after hibernation, into the yellow-brown forms (f. *levana* L.). There are also other examples of this phenemenon, e.g. among the Whites, Yellows, Satyrids and Blues.

Geographical Variability

It has already been said that the climatic factors cause different types of variability in butterflies. If the original continuity of the distribution area of some species was interrupted in the remote past by geological changes and climate fluctuation (e.g. glacier formation) the isolated populations continued to develop in different ways, especially when far apart and influenced by dissimilar climatic conditions. Sometimes the populations were separated ecologically, e.g. mountain ridges interrupted the distribution of the lowland species and, conversely, the vast lowland plains prevented fusion of populations of the mountainous species. Likewise, the forests outlined the steppe population and vice-versa. The long-term isolated development under varying natural selection pressures has resulted in the present variety of geographical races or forms.

From the classification point of view the geographical forms are very important and are known as geographical races or subspecies. They inhabit their own distribution areas which differ from those of the original, nominate form. Two different geographical races cannot live in the same habitat. It is predominantly the species with a strictly localized occurrence whose distribution is discontinuous, island-like, that have the tendency to form subspecies. In central Europe this is exemplified by pronounced differences between the Alpine, Carpathian or Pyrenean populations. The origin of geographical races on the islands is similar.

DISTRIBUTION OF BUTTERFLIES

Vertical Distribution

Butterflies occur almost everywhere throughout the world. They are absent in the Arctic, Antarctic, and the high mountains covered with perpetual snow and glaciers. Information about the distribution of the butterflies in the highest mountains is fragmentary because it comes from infrequent collections during climbing expeditions.

Some species of the Satyrids were observed at altitudes of about 6000 m in Tibet; several species are known to occur at altitudes of about 4700 m in the South American Andes; butterflies have been captured in the African Kilimanjaro mountains at altitudes of about 4000 m. On the highest mountain of Iran (Demavend — 5670 m) the author observed a continuous incidence of butterflies up to altitudes of 3800 to 3900 m and isolated specimons in sheltered places even higher. On the stony summit of the Tu-Chan mountain (3950 m), Elburz, near Teheran, the Satyrids, Whites and some small butterflies have been seen. Collections of butterflies were made at altitudes between 4000 m and 4500 m in the Hindu Kush mountains. The species *Aglais kashmirensis* Koll. was found as high as 5000 m. On the basis of different observations it can be concluded that butterflies ascend in the mountains to elevations where vegetation ceases (i.e. about 5500 m). As far as the butterflies observed at higher altitudes are concerned, they are certainly stray specimens or populations migrating through the mountain passes, which are often in the perpetual snow regions. There is a case, recorded in literature on mountaineering, of an unidentified "butterfly" seen at 6300 m altitude in the Himalayas.

The European mountains do not reach heights where butterflies cannot exist, unless they are covered with constant snow, and sightings of migrant butterflies crossing glaciers have also been reported.

Horizontal Distribution

The horizontal distribution of the butterflies is better known than the vertical one. Zoogeography is an interesting, new scientific study of the distribution of animals on the Earth.

The surface of the Earth is zoogeographically divided into several territorial units known as the zoogeographical regions which do not correspond with the continents of the orthodox geographical division of the world. The main zoogeographical regions are further partitioned into subregions and zones. Although the question of demarcation of the individual zoogeographical units is not settled yet, there are six zoogeographical regions generally recognized:

1. The Palearctic Region: includes the whole of Europe, North Africa (Sahara not excepted), the temperate zones of Asia as well as the Balearic Islands, Madeira and the Canary Islands. Approximately 22,000 species of *Lepidoptera* are found in this region; 1619 of them are classified as butterflies.

2. The Nearctic Region: comprises the whole of North America including a small part of Mexico adjoining the border of the United States of America. 14,000 known species of *Lepidoptera* live in this area. The faunas of these two large regions have much in common owing to their former common origin. Sometimes, the two regions are referred to as the Holarctic Region.

3. The Ethiopian Region: includes the part of Africa south of the Sahara, the southern part of the Arabian peninsula, Socotra, Madagascar and the adjacent small islands. About 22,000 species have been reported from this region. Madagascar is considered by some scientists to be an independent region.

4. The Oriental Region: consists of southern and southeastern Asia with nearby islands and peninsulas, e.g. Formosa, the Philippines, Borneo etc.

5. The Australian Region: embraces Australia, Tasmania, New Guinea and New Zealand. Again, the opinion is still not united regarding the definition of this region. In older literature it is called the Indo-Australian Region. This term comes from the well-known work on *Lepidoptera* by Professor A. Seitz, where the area was thus divided. Altogether, about 35,000 species occur in the Oriental and Australian region.

6. The Neotropic Region: consists of South and Central America and the major part of Mexico. Approximately 45,000 species have been described in this area.

It is worth noting that the borderline districts between the individual regions contain mixed fauna showing features indigenous to the species of the two neighbouring territories.

Europe belongs to the Palearctic Region. Many authors have attempted to divide this region further but most would agree on the division of the Palearctic Region into four parts:

1. The Euro-Siberian subregion: extending north of the Pyrenees and the Alps. It comprises a substantial part of the European regions of the U.S.S.R. and Siberia.

2. The Mediterranean subregion: i.e. North Africa, Pyrenean Peninsula, southern Europe and the Near East.

3. The Central Asian subregion: including Iran, Afghanistan, southern Volga basin, southern parts of the Asian mountains of the U.S.S.R., Mongolia and North China.

4. The East Palearctic subregion: i.e. the Himalayas, central and east China, Korea, Japan, the Far East of the U.S.S.R., Amur and Ussuri regions. The smaller the subregion, the more difficult its delineation.

Zoogeography is trying to explain the distribution of animals not only at present but also in the past (paleozoogeography).

Faunistics — a subsidiary branch of zoogeography — studies the occurrence of species in a defined natural area. It also notes the changes of the animal distribution. Collectors of butterflies can make a valuable contribution to this science by gathering very important data.

Number of Butterfly Species

For many reasons it is impossible to make an exact estimation of the number of butterfly species living on the Earth. There are still extensive territories in the world where the distribution of butterflies has only been elucidated in part or not at all. In contrast to this, the deeper knowledge of the life of butterflies and their anatomy now permits us to separate even very closely related species that were previously considered to be one.

The number of butterfly species in individual European countries shows the following pattern: 39 species occur in Ireland, 69 in Great Britain, 115 in Sweden and 114 in Finland. Only 5 species of butterflies have been reported from Greenland. The number of species in central Europe is increasing. For example 172 species are found in Czechoslovakia and about 200 in East and West Germany. The butterfly fauna of France is enriched by the Mediterranean species. It is estimated that there are 230 species in France. The overall number of the known European species now total 355. Some species are observed in all European countries, other inhabit only certain areas that fulfill their ecological requirements (e.g. the mountain species of the Alps the species of northern Europe favouring low temperatures, the Mediterranean species, etc.). The determination of the number of geographical races is very difficult but it seems that there are at least several thousands of them.

SIGNIFICANCE OF BUTTERFLIES AND MOTHS IN NATURE

It must be understood that terms like significance, usefulness, damage, beauty, etc., are strange to nature. They were invented by man to serve his ends. There is nothing static in nature; everything is constantly changing under the influence of natural selection. Any creature which cannot compete must die and is replaced by a new form. Despite all this, human society classifies butterflies as economically useful, injurious and indifferent. Most butterflies are indifferent while most of the useful and injurious species are found among the moths.

Useful Species

The adult lepidopterous insects are very often useful pollinators although not as important as the bees, bumble-bees and similar insects. The Silkworm is absolutely essential for the silk industry. Some species of caterpillars, feeding exclusively on weeds, have been used in weed control, i.e. they are artificially introduced into areas infested with weeds. The well-known American Cactus Moth *(Cactoblastis cactorum* Berg.), whose caterpillars feed on the opuntia, was employed to control the rampant opuntias in Australia.

Pests

A number of species among *Lepidoptera* cause damage. Their caterpillars endanger crops, fruit and forest trees. Every farmer is familiar with the damage which may be caused by the Dart Moth caterpillar known as the "Cutworm", by the caterpillars of the Silver Y Moth, Cabbage Moth etc., in the sugar-beet and vegetable fields. The Gipsy Moth and the

Antler Moth also frequently cause damage. Almost everybody knows the moths feeding on stored food or penetrating into wardrobes and bee-hives. The Tussock Moths and the Leaf Rollers do considerable damage to deciduous forests. Fruit trees are not spared and their leaves, buds and fruits are destroyed. The Goat-moths and their allies live inside plants and bore into the roots, thus ruining the plants, spoiling wood, and predisposing them to fungal diseases.

Most of the pests belong to the moth species but among the butterflies also there are some that cause damage. Particularly infamous are the caterpillars of the Large White, which can be a real disaster for garden and field vegetables during summer and autumn. In more southerly parts of central Europe the Black-veined White causes damage to the fruit trees, and from time to time, the Large Tortoiseshell attacks the foliage of cherry and pear trees in spring.

Indifferent Species

The above-mentioned examples show that the activities and importance of butterflies are not always very clear. Some species are useful or injurious; most of them are, however, indifferent and their significance cannot be measured in economic terms. Is it possible to talk about being harmful or beneficial when considering caterpillars that feed on the stinging nettle, dog violet, blackthorn, dock and other wild plants? Can the butterflies living high up in the mountains, in the peat-bogs or on sandy and stony steppes be useful or harmful in any way? All the same, these species are not insignificant to man; their existence or non-existence show whether "things are going right" in the natural environment. The number of butterflies is decreasing, and this is an alarming sign of dangerous forces at work on our external environment.

ENEMIES AND DISEASES OF BUTTERFLIES

The females of many species lay dozens or even thousands of eggs; the quantity of butterflies is not increasing — rather the opposite. This fact can be easily accounted for because butterflies, like other animals, suffer from various diseases and parasite infections, and are hunted by predators. The pollution of the environment also threatens their existence. Butterflies and their developmental stages serve as food to insectivorous vertebrates and invertebrates and are subject to virus, bacterial and fungal diseases.

Virus Diseases

Polyedria is the most notorious virus disease affecting caterpillars. The diseased caterpillars climb up into the tree tops where they stay limp, hanging upside down. In a short time their gut turns to a foul smelling thin brown liquid. Another type of virus disease — granulosis — is a subject of research, especially in relationship to economically important species both useful and injurious. Many butterflies, e.g. the Painted Lady, Large White, Clouded Yellows and some Nymphalids suffer from these and similar diseases.

Bacterial Diseases and Microsporidia

Caterpillars are liable to bacterial diseases. The illness caused by *Bacillus thuringiensis* Berliner is the most notorious. The caterpillar picks up the disease from infected food and this fact is made use of in biological control of pests — plants are sprayed with a suspension containing pathogen. This microbe is harmless to man and other vertebrates, unlike many of the chemical agents used so extensively nowadays.

The Microsporidia belong to the large group of the protozoal agents of diseases. They attack individual organs but may also cause a general illness. Well-known is the Silkworm disease caused by *Nosema bombycis* Nägeli; this illness was also studied by L. Pasteur. Related disease of butterflies (the Large White, Small White, Black-veined White) is caused by *Nosema messnili* Paillot. Species of the *Nosema* group are lethal to many butterfly caterpillars.

Fungal Diseases

Caterpillars infected by viruses or bacteria initially go soft and later liquefy. Fungal diseases of caterpillars run a different course. The caterpillars attacked by the fungus *Tarichium megaspermum* Cohn become yellow at first, later turning brownish, and finally completely black. Inside the caterpillar, under the skin, the spores appear which then fill up the whole body. The Tarichium fungus destroys especially the caterpillars of moths.

Another common fungal disease is caused by *Beauveria bassiana* Bals., which infects the caterpillars of the Small White. Practical utilization of fungal diseases as a means of biological control of caterpillars has not been worked out in the same detail as it has been in the case of bacterial conditions.

Predators and Other Enemies

Butterflies are pursued by a great number of predacious and parasitic insects and other invertebrates. The Robber-flies are formidable predators of butterflies. They are large flies, sitting still on tree trunks, logs or branches on summer days, lurking, ready to hunt their prey. As soon as a butterfly or other insect appears in the vicinity, the Robber-fly starts off immediately, attacks in the air and takes its prey to a suitable place to suck it dry. Spiders, too, are hunters of butterflies. They assault them on flowers, in the grass or among the leaves of shrubs.

Caterpillars have the greatest number of enemies. There are a particularly large number of beetle predators that attack them. In deciduous forests on the Continent where the Gipsy Moth sometimes increases unduly, a corresponding increase in the number of the predatory beetle *(Calosoma sycophanta* L.*)* is observed. These are beautiful, relatively large beetles, with metallic greenish-mauve wing-covers. They actively hunt caterpillars on the ground and on the branches of trees, often assisted by the Rove Beetles as well as other predatory species. The Four-Spotted Carrion Beetle *(Xylodrepa quadripunctata* L.*)* with conspicuous dark spots on the yellow-brown wing-covers is another ardent pursuer of small caterpillars. Both the imago and larva of this beetle feed on caterpillars. Even ants are enemies of butterflies and caterpillars.

The most numerous and important enemies of caterpillars are the Ichneumons, Braconids and Chalcids, inhabiting meadows, fields, woodland and steppes. Hundreds of different species are known. They approach the caterpillar, inject their eggs into it by means of the ovipositor and fly off looking for another victim. When the larvae hatch from the eggs, they feed on the fat deposits of the caterpillar leaving the vital organs intact, so that the caterpillar is wasting away but still growing, and sometimes even succeeds in pupating. But instead of a beautiful butterfly, the parasite emerges from the pupa. Some of the hymenopterous insects attack the eggs of butterflies. Several important parasitic species are found among the True Flies. The Caterpillar Fly *(Tachinidae)* for example, glues its eggs onto the caterpillar's skin; later, having hatched, the small larvae bite their way into the body of the caterpillar, and live inside it.

Among vertebrates, the most dangerous enemies of the butterflies are the birds and the insectivorous mammals.

Defence of Butterflies Against Their Enemies

Although most *Lepidoptera* are comparatively defenceless, many species possess efficient deterrent and defensive mechanisms that can often save them from their enemies. They are able to escape the onslaught of a bird by a rapid zig-zagging flight. When a Nymphalid settles on a tree trunk it closes its wings to hide the bright colours and thus merges with the background; its protective coloration is a very efficacious defensive device.

The caterpillars also have ways of defending themselves. They are perfectly camouflaged, some of them completely fusing with the surrounding environment. There are caterpillars containing chemicals in their bodies which are distasteful to insect-eating animals. Some species of moths build large nests among the branches of trees and shrubs where they live all their life, or at least when young and vulnerable. The nests protect the caterpillars not only from enemies but also from the fluctuations of temperature and humidity and they leave it only temporarily to get food.

The Roman numerals which appear in the top
right-hand column refer to the months of the year
when the butterfly (or its contingent 2nd and 3rd generation),
caterpillar and pupa are generally to be found.

Swallowtail

Papilionidae

Papilio machaon LINNAEUS, 1758

The Swallowtail is undoubtedly one of the best known species of the butterflies in Europe. It does not occur in Ireland and in England it is rare and local, its range of distribution being limited only to the Norfolk Broads. Its occurrence in central Europe has also decreased markedly during recent decades, although it is still quite abundant in some areas. The Swallowtail occurs in North Africa, Europe, the temperate zone of Asia and some parts of North America. It is found high up in the mountains, even at altitudes of about 2000 m in the Alps and 4500 m in Tibet.

A great number of types and geographical races have been described. The home of the *gorganus* Fruhstorfer subspecies is central Europe, that of the *britannicus* Seitz subspecies is England, and that of the *aliaska* Scudder and two other subspecies is North America. The caterpillar has a very variegated appearance. When disturbed, it protrudes from the front part of the body a fleshy orange-red forked organ called the osmeterium. The pupa is usually green or grey-brown. In central Europe the pupal stage lasts two or three weeks. In hibernating pupae it may last six months. In the mountains and in northern regions the butterfly has only one generation a year.

Butterfly: IV.—VI.; VII.—VIII., in the south a part of the third generation (IX.—X.). *Caterpillar:* VI.; VII.—IX., sometimes also X. *Foodplants:* Fennel, carrot, dill, celery, parsley, and a number of other umbelliferous plants. In the Near East an allied species causes damage to citrus trees.

1 — caterpillar,
2 — adult,
3 — pupa

1

2

3

Scarce Swallowtail

Iphiclides podalirius LINNAEUS, 1758

The Scarce Swallowtail is found in gardens, fields, open woodlands. You can come across it in places with sloe thickets and particularly orchards. It is widespread throughout Europe with the exceptions of the northern parts. Its range extends northwards to Saxony and central Poland and eastwards across Asia Minor and Transcaucasia as far as Iran and western China. A few specimens of the Scarce Swallowtail have been reported from central Sweden and England but they were probably only strays and not migrants. In the Alps it can be found up to altitudes of 1600 m. In some years the Scarce Swallowtail is quite abundant. The caterpillars spin little pads on leaves and grip them firmly. The newly hatched caterpillar is dark in colour with two smaller and two bigger greenish patches on the dorsal side, later they are greenish with yellowish dorsal and side stripes. The summer chrysalides are green as a rule, the hibernating ones are brown. A number of hibernating chrysalides fall prey to various enemies. The Scarce Swallowtail is getting rarer as the blackthorn bushes are being cleared; and it is now protected in some central European countries.

Butterfly:
End of IV. — beginning of VI.; VII. — beginning of IX.
Caterpillar:
V.—IX. (development takes about 5—8 weeks).
Foodplants:
Blackthorn, hawthorn, bird cherry and fruit trees. Chrysalis hibernates. The stage of chrysalis lasts 3—5 weeks, the extremes being 7 days to one year.

1 — adult,
2 — caterpillar,
3 — *f. undecimlineatus* Eim. adult,
4 — pupa

1

2

3

4

Southern Festoon

Zerynthia polyxena SCHIFFERMÜLLER, 1775

Spanish Festoon
Zerynthia rumina LINNAEUS, 1758

The Southern Festoon is found in southern and south-eastern Europe and penetrates even to its central parts. The species was first described near Vienna. From the total of about twenty geographical races described, the best known is the *cassandra* Hübner ssp. from the south-western part of the Southern Festoon's distribution. The butterfly is not shy, and flutters close to the ground. It often rests on flowers and grass stalks. The caterpillar is many-coloured. Its development takes about 4—5 weeks. It feeds on different species of *Aristolochia*. The chrysalis is brownish and rather stick-like.

The Spanish Festoon occurs in the western Mediterranean regions. Its distribution area extends from Briançon, along the Riviera as far as Spain and Portugal. It is also native in North Africa, where the ssp. *ornatior* Blach. was described. Hilly regions and the maritime mountains are the most usual places where it occurs.

Z. polyxena:
IV.—VI.
Caterpillar:
V.—VII.
Chrysalis hibernates.
Foodplants of both species:
Various species of *Aristolochia*.
Z. rumina:
II.—V.
according to the altitude of locality.
Caterpillar:
III.—VI.
Chrysalis hibernates.

Z. polyxena:
1 — adult,
2 — caterpillar,
4 — pupa
Z. rumina:
3 — adult

Clouded Apollo

Parnassius mnemosyne LINNAEUS, 1758

This butterfly inhabits meadows and woodland clearings with plenty of flowering plants, both in the lowlands and in the mountains. It is not usually found at altitudes above 1500 m except in the Asian mountains where it is known also from higher altitudes. It does not occur in Ireland, England, Portugal, or Spain. Its range of distribution extends from the Pyrenees, across the Central Massif, the Alps, and the Carpathians as far as central Asia. It inhabits all European countries including Norway, where it appears rarely and only in certain places. A great number of different geographical races and individual forms are distinguished in this extensive region. The most striking specimens include the dark race from the eastern Bavarian Alps (ssp. *hartmanni* Stdf.); f. *melaina* Hon. has the most pronounced dark colouring. The Clouded Apollo is quite common in some places in central Europe but the inhabited areas are strictly limited in size. The female lays whitish eggs with a granular surface. The caterpillar feeds only on sunny days, otherwise it is hidden under leaves or stones. The blunt-ended chrysalis lies on the ground in a light spun covering. To prevent the continuing disappearance of this butterfly from many places in central Europe, it is now protected in some regions.

Butterfly:
V.—VII.
Caterpillar:
IV.—VI.
(according to altitude).
Foodplants:
Various species of fumewort (*Corydalis*).
Hibernates in the egg stage.

1 — male,
2 — female,
3 — caterpillar,
4 — ssp.
hartmanni f. *melaina*

Apollo

Parnassius apollo LINNAEUS, 1758

The Apollo is indubitably one of the prettiest butterflies and for this reason it is very much sought after by collectors. Its popularity is partly due to its immense variability. About six hundred different forms have already been described. The Apollo inhabits valleys, hillsides and mountain meadows. In the Alps it is found at altitudes of about 2200 m and in the Asian mountains even higher. The vast area of its distribution includes the Pyrenean peninsula, the Alps, the Carpathians and the Caucasus, extending as far east as the Altai mountains. It is not found in Ireland or in Britain. In some parts of central Europe it has disappeared entirely or is getting noticeably rare; it is therefore protected in a number of European countries. It flies slowly, flutteringly and gliding, and likes to settle on flowering thistles. It is not shy. The full grown caterpillar is up to 50 mm long. It is velvet black with small steel blue raised dots and flanked with many orange spots. The chrysalis stage lasts from eight days to several weeks. The fat, blunt-ended pupa is tinted blue.

Butterfly:
VI.—IX., in central Europe VII.—VIII.
Caterpillar:
VIII.—VI. or III.—VI.; sometimes hibernates; is heliophillic, i.e. in the absence of sunshine it hides under stones and does not feed.
Foodplants:
Houseleek and various species of stonecrop, etc.

1 — male,
2 — female,
3 — caterpillar

Large White

Pieris brassicae LINNAEUS, 1758

The Large White is widespread throughout Europe, in North Africa and even as far east as the Himalayas. Most often it can be found in gardens, but it also inhabits fields, meadows, woodland margins and mountain valleys. The female lays two to three hundred orange-yellow eggs, which are glued in clusters to the underside of leaves. The caterpillar hatches after four to ten days; it starts to eat the leaves from the centre, only beginning to nibble the edges several days later. It moults four or five times during its development, which lasts three to four weeks or sometimes even longer, depending on the climatic conditions of the habitat. Before pupating, caterpillars leave the foodplant and search for sheltered places in the neighbourhood. They pupate underneath window ledges and the eaves of houses, on fences, milestones, etc. The pupa is usually yellow-green with dark spots. Among the caterpillars preparing for pupation there are always a number which are killed by the parasitic larvae of the Braconid wasp *(Apanteles glomeratus* L.*)*. Instead of turning into a pupa, the caterpillar dies, surrounded by the yellow cocoons of the parasites which have been feeding inside its body.

Butterfly:
IV. — beginning of VI., half of VII.—VIII.; partial 3rd generation in IX.—X.
Caterpillar:
VI.—VIII.; VIII.—IX.
Main foodplants:
Cauliflower, cabbage, radish, cress, etc.
In central and northern Europe it causes damage to vegetable production.
Pupa hibernates.

1— female,
2 — underside of wings (female),
3 — male,
4 — caterpillar,
5 — pupa

1

2

3

4

5

Small White

Pieris rapae LINNAEUS, 1758

The Small White is one of the commonest and most abundant of the butterflies. Its area of distribution extends from the British Isles and North Africa as far as Japan. It has been introduced even to North America, Australia, Hawaii, New Zealand and Tasmania. It is a dangerous pest in some places. In central Europe two to three generations occur not strictly separated in time, whereas there is only one generation in populations living in high mountains. The spring form is easily distinguished from the summer one. It is usually smaller with less distinct pattern. A great number of different forms have been described. The female seldom lays more than one or two eggs at a time, the total number being 150—200. After hatching, the caterpillar devours its egg shell. Then it starts feeding on the surface of the leaves, making irregular holes in them. It pupates after the fourth moulting. The pupal stage lasts 7 to 10 days — in hibernating pupae up to ten months. It is easy to breed these caterpillars in captivity and they are often used in scientific experiments. In nature the caterpillars and pupae are often infested with parasites of the orders *Hymenoptera* and *Diptera*.

Butterfly:
III.—X.
Caterpillar:
III.—IX.
Foodplants:
Various species of *Brassica*, mignonette, etc. In some places it is a pest on cabbages. The chrysalis hibernates.

1 — underside of wings (female),
2 — male,
3 — female,
4 — caterpillar,
5 — f. *flavida* Pet. (yellow form)

Green-veined White

Pieris napi LINNAEUS, 1758

This butterfly is widely distributed and in some regions quite abundant. It occurs throughout Europe and the temperate zones of Asia, in North Africa and North America. The variability of this species is outstanding; a tremendous number of different forms and geographical races have been described. In central Europe it usually develops two generations and a partial third one. Butterflies of the different generations vary markedly in their appearance. The Green-veined White is found in fields, gardens, meadows, along woodland margins and in clearings and mountain valleys. The female lays her eggs singly. The caterpillar hatches in 4 to 6 days. After hatching it devours the egg shell and later starts to feed on the surface of leaves. It does not eat the leaf edges until it is fully grown. Its development lasts two to three weeks, during which time it moults four times. The Green-veined White only rarely becomes a pest. The pupa is greyish or green. The pupal stage lasts a week to ten days; in hibernating pupae about ten months.

Butterfly:
III.—X.
Caterpillar:
III.—X.
(duration of development takes 2—3 weeks).
Foodplants:
Turnip, wild cabbage, hedge-mustard, radish, bittercress, pepperwort, etc. Chrysalis hibernates.

1 — male,
2 — female,
3 — caterpillar,
4 — underside of wings,
5 — pupa,
6 — f. *hybernica* Sch.

Dark-veined White

Pieris bryoniae HÜBNER, 1806

The Dark-veined White is one of the butterflies very much sought after by many collectors, particularly in Austria. This is because one of the most variable populations of this butterfly lives in the well-known Mödling area near Vienna. There has been a long debate among experts as to whether it is an independent species or only a subspecies of the Green-veined White. Sometimes it is considered to be a semispecies, modification, variety, etc. The author had the opportunity to observe populations of the Dark-veined White in the Carpathians and the Alps and is of the opinion that it is an independent species. The nominate form has been described in the Alps, where it is found at considerable altitudes (up to 2000 m) and has only one generation a year. Both pairs of the female's wings are dark. At lower altitudes two or three generations appear during a year. Ssp. *neobryoniae* Shelj., resembling most closely the Carpathian populations, lives in the southern parts of the Alps and the ssp. *flavescens* Wagner inhabits the northern parts. The ground coloration of the wings is yellowish or rich yellow, often with a mauve gloss. The populations inhabiting the Carpathians are very varied. The most distinct ones include the ssp. *vihorlatensis* Moucha found in Vihorlat, the east Slovakian mountains.

Butterfly:
V., VI.—VII., partial third generation in VIII. In mountain regions the only generation flies VI.—VII., the time of occurrence depends on the altitude of habitat.
Caterpillar:
From V. to IX.
Foodplants: Rock-cress, wild-mustard, penny-cress.

1 — male,
2 — ssp. *flavescens* (female),
3 — ssp. *vihorlatensis* (female),
4 — female,
5 — ssp. *neobryoniae* (female)

Bath White

Pontia daplidice LINNAEUS, 1758

While some of the species of the Whites migrate only occasionally, the Bath White is a regular traveller. This is particularly apparent in the natural conditions of central and western Europe. The spring generation strongly differs from the summer one and even has its own name. In Europe the area inhabited by the species extends to 66° N. Only stray specimens are reported from Ireland and Norway. The species is more often found in England, but even there it is a comparatively rare migrant only. The total range of its distribution includes North Africa, southern Europe and most of the temperate zone of Asia. In some years the Bath White is quite abundant in central Europe while in others it is quite rare, this fluctuation depending on the intensity of migration in respective years. The egg stage is short; it lasts only 7 to 8 days. A continuous succession of generations during one year is known from the southern regions of its distribution area. In central Europe two generations appear, with fewer individuals in spring than in summer. The difference between butterflies of the two generations can be clearly seen in the illustrations.

Butterfly:
IV.—V.;
VII.—VIII. (in the south II.—X.).
Caterpillar:
III.—X. (in central Europe mainly V.—VI.).
Foodplants:
Wild mignonette, mustard and different species of the cress family. Chrysalis hibernates. Very abundant in some places in southern Europe.

1 — gen.
vern. *bellidice* O. (spring form),
2 — male,
3 — female,
4 — underside of wings

Orange Tip

Anthocharis cardamines LINNAEUS, 1758

The Orange Tip is a lovely butterfly of spring meadows, fields and forest pathways. The male can be easily recognized at a considerable distance by the conspicuous orange patches on its forewings. This species has only one generation in central Europe. In the Alps it can be found even at altitudes exceeding 2000 m. The distribution area of the Orange Tip includes the whole of the palearctic region from the British Isles to Japan where, however, it is very rare; it was discovered there as late as 1910 by the collector Nakamura. The female lays eggs on the underside of leaves and also often on flowers. The egg is barrel-shaped with 11 to 13 grooves on its surface. At first yellow-white, it turns orange and then grey before hatching in about two weeks. The development of the caterpillar takes approximately five weeks. In captivity it has often been possible to breed a second generation which also appears spontaneously in the individuals inhabiting the south of Europe. The pupa is usually attached to the stalk of a foodplant. The newly pupated chrysalis is green and later turns buff. In rare cases the pupa maintains its green colour until the imago has emerged.

Butterfly:
IV.—VI. (in the mountains also VII.).
Caterpillar:
V.—VIII.
Foodplants:
Great variety of plants, e. g. garlic mustard, rock-cress, lady's smock, penny-cress. Chrysalis hibernates.

1 — male,
2 — female,
3 — caterpillar,
4 — pupa,
5 — underside of wings

1

2

3

4

5

Wood White

Leptidea sinapis LINNAEUS, 1758

Fenton's Wood White
Leptidea morsei FENTON, 1881

The Wood White is an inconspicuous butterfly of woodland clearings, rides and margins. The first brood appears when the blackthorn is in flower, the other during the summer months. In the Alps it is found as high as 1900 m. This species is widespread almost in the whole of Europe with the exception of Scotland and Malta, and in the Netherlands it is rather rare. The development of the caterpillar takes about three weeks. The pupa hibernates.

Fenton's Wood White was discovered in Europe as late as the beginning of this century, originally described as a separate form of the Wood White. However, it differs from this by the shape of the wings, particularly the forewings, and also by the size, and colouring of the underside, which is never such a rich yellow as it is in the Wood White. This form was originally described as ab. *major* Grund. Professor Z. Lorković has found, however, that the form in question is in fact a geographical race of the white *Leptidea morsei*, already known from Asia. The western borderline of its distribution area goes through Moravia, Slovakia and Austria.

L. sinapis:
IV.—VI.;
VI.—VIII.
Caterpillar:
V.—IX.
Foodplants:
Birdsfoot trefoil, sweet pea, crown vetch, milk vetch.

L. morsei:
IV.—VI.;
VI.—VII.
Caterpillar:
V.—VIII.
Foodplant:
Sweet pea.

L. sinapis:
1 — male,
2 — female,
3 — underside of wings,
4 — pupa,
5 — caterpillar
L. morsei:
6 — underside of wings,
7— male

Black-veined White

Aporia crataegi LINNAEUS, 1758

In the 19th century the Black-veined White used to be a serious pest in orchards in central Europe. During the last few decades it has become much rarer and can be found in great numbers only in the southern and south-eastern parts of central Europe, in the Balkan Peninsula and in Asia Minor. The caterpillars cause considerable damage to fruit trees. When disturbed they let themselves down on fine silk-like threads. After the second moulting they attain the size of about half a centimetre. They then go into hibernation in a nest constructed of leaves and thin twigs spun together. From April of the following year the caterpillars continue to damage fruit trees. In the latter half of May they are fully grown. The pupa is attached to a branch or stem. The Black-veined White occurs throughout most of central and southern Europe, North Africa and the temperate part of Asia including the Far East. It is gradually disappearing in Europe and has become quite extinct in England, where it was last seen in about 1925.

Butterfly:
V.—VII.
Caterpillar:
VII.—VI.
Foodplants:
Fruit trees, hawthorn, blackthorn, etc. Development including hibernation takes ten months. Pupa is found from IV. to VII. depending on the altitude of habitat. The stage of pupa lasts 2—5 weeks.

1 — caterpillar,
2 — pupa,
3 — male,
4 — female

Berger's Clouded Yellow

Colias australis VERITY, 1911

Pale Clouded Yellow

Colias hyale LINNAEUS, 1758

Berger's Clouded Yellow has been described as a separate species only recently. The Italian researcher R. Verity described it in Andalusia, Spain, but it was not until after the second World War that its area of distribution was definitely found to include also western and central Europe, approximately to 53°N. Up to now Berger's Clouded Yellow has been found in England, in the Netherlands, in Poland and in all countries of central Europe, where it is very common in some places, particularly in habitats with a limestone setting. It flies about from spring until late autumn. The butterfly has two or three generations a year. The ground colouring of the male is rich yellow, the wings having a less pronounced grey tinge at the base than those of the Pale Clouded Yellow. The outer edge of the forewings is more conspicuously rounded. The ground colouring of the female is whitish with a greenish tint.

The Pale Clouded Yellow occurs also in the north, e.g. near Leningrad, in Finland, and central Sweden. In the Alps it is found even at altitudes of about 2000 m. Both species have a similar way of life, sometimes occurring together in one locality. As opposed to the butterflies, which have a marked resemblance, the caterpillars can be easily distinguished.

C. australis: End of IV.—VI.; VII.—VIII.; IX.—X. (only two generations in northern part of the distribution area).
Caterpillar: From V.
Foodplants: Crown vetch and horseshoe vetch.

C. hyale: End of IV. or beginning of V.—VI.; VII.—VIII.; IX.—X.
Caterpillar: From V.
Foodplants: Lucerne, crown vetch and other plants of the family *Papilionaceae.* Caterpillar hibernates in both species.

C. hyale:
1 — male
C. australis:
2 — male,
3 — underside of wings,
4 — female

Moorland Clouded Yellow

Pieridae

Colias palaeno LINNAEUS, 1761

This species should be protected everywhere in central Europe. Draining of the countryside and the cutting of peat has resulted in the extinction of the butterfly in many places where it used to be common. The whole distribution area of the Moorland Clouded Yellow extends from western and central Europe as far as Japan, but it has been reported also from North America. Its distribution is, however, discontinuous as the butterfly is only found in places with abundant growth of the caterpillar's foodplant. Many geographical races have been described. The nominate form occurs in Scandinavia; ssp. *europome* Esper, 1779, described in Saxony, lives in central Europe. Another of the outstanding forms is *illgneri* Rühl, the female only, in which the ground colouring of the wings is yellowish instead of whitish. In the Alps the species is found locally at altitudes of about 2500 m. The high mountain populations usually have a narrower black margin of wings interspersed with light dots in the female.

The female lays greenish-yellow eggs, which later become reddish and turn grey before the hatching of the caterpillar. The egg stage lasts about a week. The caterpillar feeds during the daytime. It hibernates after the second moulting.

Butterfly:
VI.—VII.
Caterpillar:
VI.—V.
Foodplants:
Bog bilberry.
Stage of pupa lasts 1—3 weeks, usually V. and VI.

1 — male,
2 — female,
3 — caterpillar,
4 — f. *illgneri*

Clouded Yellow

Pieridae

Colias crocea FOURCROY, 1785

The abundance of the Clouded Yellow in central and western Europe in some years, in contrast to its relative rarity in others, can be easily explained by the fact that it is a migrant species. Its occurrence in a given year depends on its migration from the south. The most precise records of the migration intensity come from Great Britain. It is quite difficult to define the exact boundary of the permanent occurrence of this species in Europe. It is probably formed by the Alps and the Carpathians, north of which the species is mostly migrant. The Clouded Yellow inhabits North Africa, Asia, including Iran and Asia Minor. In southern Europe it is not uncommon. In exceptional cases it spreads northwards even to Sweden and Finland. The butterfly shows comparatively little variability. Only the size and number of the orange dots on the outer margin of the forewings of the female sometimes fluctuates. Of the commonly occurring forms it is particularly f. *helice* Hb. that deserves being mentioned. The development of the caterpillar takes about two to five weeks and up to ten months when hibernating, so that the caterpillar may be found in all months of the year.

Butterfly:
Arrival to western and central Europe coincides with end of IV.—VI., in which case the butterfly is found until X. in 2—3 generations.
Foodplants:
Lucerne, clover, trefoil, melilot, vetch, crown vetch, etc. Caterpillar hibernates.

1 — male,
2 — female,
3 — female f. *helice*,
4 — caterpillar,
5 — pupa

Brimstone

Gonepteryx rhamni LINNAEUS, 1758

Although this species shows only small variability, eleven subspecies have so far been designated, apart from the nominate subspecies only one of them living in Europe. The Brimstone is widespread throughout North Africa and western Europe, extending through Asia Minor and Asia proper as far as the eastern parts of the palearctic region. The Brimstone is well known in western and central Europe especially because the butterfly hibernates and leaves its winter shelter early in spring, when there are still the last remnants of snow lying in the shaded places. The next generation of butterflies hatches out in June or early July and they can be seen on the wing until September, when they go into hibernation. The eggs are not laid until the spring, when the buckthorn bushes begin to come into leaf. The individuals that have hibernated may be found up to the end of May and at higher altitudes even later. Its distribution in time fluctuates, according to climatic conditions and the altitude of habitat. The development of the green caterpillar lasts three to seven weeks. It feeds on leaves, initially eating the centres and later nibbling the edges. The pupa hangs in the tree from a leaf or twig and is very well camouflaged.

Butterfly:
From VI. to V. next year.
Caterpillar:
V.—VIII. Partial second generation in VII.—IX. in North Africa.
Foodplant:
Buckthorn.

1 — male,
2 — underside of wings,
3 — pupa,
4 — caterpillar,
5 — female

Lesser Purple Emperor

Apatura ilia SCHIFFERMÜLLER, 1775

Nymphalidae

This butterfly, as well as the Purple Emperor, resembles the brightly coloured tropical species. Light reflection on the scales of the male's forewings causes a pretty violet-blue iridescence. The Lesser Purple Emperor is widespread throughout western and central Europe, across Asia Minor and the temperate zone of the palearctic region as far as Japan, in which area several geographical races can be distinguished. It does not occur in England nor in some of the islands in the Mediterranean. One of the best known forms is f. *clytie* Schiffermüller with yellow spots in the corners of the forewings, illustrated here. In some places this form is much more abundant than the nominate one, originally described near Vienna. The Lesser Purple Emperor is most commonly found by ponds and streams where the foodplants of the caterpillar grow. It lives both in lowlands and in the hills, but it avoids higher mountains. A second generation may occur in southern Europe; in central Europe only one generation is the rule.

Butterfly:
V.—VII. (in the south also VIII.—IX.).
Caterpillar:
VII.—V.
Foodplants:
Aspen, poplar, sallow, various species of willow, etc. Pupal stage lasts 2—3 weeks; it is usually found in VI. Caterpillar hibernates.

1 — male,
2 — male
f. *clytie*,
3 — caterpillar

1

2

3

Purple Emperor

Nymphalidae

Apatura iris LINNAEUS, 1758

The area of distribution of this species ranges from England throughout the whole of the temperate zone of the palearctic region as far as Japan. The butterfly inhabits deciduous woods and is also found along streams. It likes to settle on muddy woodland rides to drink. Both species of the European Emperor are shy butterflies, and for this reason they are not easy to capture. The butterfly loses its shyness when thirsty. The Purple Emperor is one of the very common butterflies in some parts of deciduous forests in Europe. It flies about woodland rides, where it can find horse dung and carrion, which attract these beautiful butterflies from the whole neighbourhood. It prefers lowlands and is only rarely found at altitudes of more than 1300 m. As a rule, only the males are captured, as the females stay at the tops of high trees. The female glues her eggs to willow leaves. The caterpillar is at first brown, later turning green with yellowish spots and a side stripe. It hibernates after the second moulting. The best known and most conspicuous form is f. *iole* Schiffermüller, which lacks most of the white markings.

Butterfly:
VI.—VIII.
Caterpillar:
VIII.—V.
Foodplants:
Various species of willow and aspen.
It hibernates in a spun nest on a twig or a leaf near a bud. The pupal stage lasts 2—3 weeks; it is usually found in VI.

1 — male,
2 — male
f. *iole*,
3 — caterpillar,
4 — pupa

Common Glider

Neptis sappho PALLAS, 1771

Hungarian Glider
Neptis rivularis SCOPOLI, 1763

Both species had their Latin names changed several times recently and it cannot be guaranteed that the present classification of this genus will not undergo further changes in nomenclature. Fortunately, the two species can be easily distinguished by means of the white wing design, as shown in the illustration. In their wide distribution area they both form a number of geographical races. The Common Glider is widespread throughout eastern Europe and penetrates through extensive regions of central Asia as far as Japan. The western boundary of its area passes through Austria and northern Yugoslavia. The species description was made according to the specimens found in the Volga basin. The caterpillar is yellow-brown, the pupa yellow with two protrusions. The pupa of the spring generation has shiny metallic spots.

The Hungarian Glider has a similar range of distribution but it is more likely to be found along woodland margins, as opposed to the former species, which prefers shrubby hillsides and heathland. The western boundary passes through regions similar to those of the Common Glider. The caterpillar is red-brown with light stripes, the pupa is short, light brown with two protrusions.

N. sappho:
V.—VI.;
VII.—IX.
Caterpillar:
VI.—V. (some of the caterpillars pupate the same year and produce butterflies of the second generation).
Foodplant:
Spring vetchling.

N. rivularis:
V.—VII. (sometimes also VIII.) in one generation.
Caterpillar:
Until the end of V.
Foodplants:
Different species of the *Spiraea*. Both species hibernate as caterpillars.

N. sappho:
1 — underside of wings,
3 — adult
N. rivularis:
2 — underside of wings,
4 — adult

White Admiral
Limenitis camilla LINNAEUS, 1763

Southern White Admiral
Limenitis reducta STAUDINGER, 1901

The two species look much alike but still they can be easily distinguished. The White Admiral has two rows of black spots on the outer underside margin of the hindwing in contrast to the Southern White Admiral, which has only one.

The White Admiral occurs all over central Europe as well as in England and southern Sweden, penetrating as far as Japan. It is found in woodland rides and clearings and in the Alps reaches altitudes of about 1500 m. Generally, single specimens are to be seen, only in some localities do they appear in larger numbers. The caterpillar is yellow-green with white dots and brown bristles. The pupa is green with two small horns on its head and spattered with silvery spots.

The Southern White Admiral inhabits the sunlit scrub-covered hillsides and forest margins. It occurs in southern Europe, Asia Minor, Transcaucasia and Iran. In some places it is fairly abundant and regularly has two generations during one year. Only one generation appears along the northern boundary of its distribution, which passes through central Europe. In the south it produces up to three consecutive generations in a year. On the southern slopes of the Alps it is found at altitudes of about 1300 m. The caterpillar has two rows of red spikes. The pupa is grey-brown with metallic spots.

L. camilla:
V.—VII.;
Caterpillar:
VII.—V.

L. reducta:
V.—IX. (usually in two generations).
Caterpillar:
VII.—V.
Foodplants:
Caterpillars of both species feed on different species of honeysuckle. They pupate after hibernation, usually in V. The pupal stage lasts less than two weeks.

L. camilla:
1 — adult,
2 — underside of wings
L. reducta:
3 — underside of wings,
4 — adult

Poplar Admiral

Nymphalidae

Limenitis populi LINNAEUS, 1758

The ground coloration of the male is dark brown or black. It has a few white spots on the forewing and several brick-red half-moons along the outer margin of the wings. The ground colouring of the underside is light brown and the white spots have grey-green or bluish iridescence. Sometimes it is possible to come across a male without the white spots on the upperside of the wings (f. *tremulae* Esp.); in some places it is even more common than the nominate form. The female has a much more conspicuous white design particularly on the hindwings. The Poplar Admiral inhabits deciduous and mixed forests of almost the entire temperate zone of Eurasia. It is widespread in central Europe but never found in large numbers. It is rare in the Netherlands and Denmark and does not occur in Great Britain. The butterfly frequents the banks of streams and rivers where the trees needed by the caterpillar grow. Most of the time the butterflies fly about at the tops of trees, coming down to the ground only to drink. They settle on muddy roads and on various kinds of decaying matter (e.g. fruit and food refuse, animal dung and carrion). The pupa is yellow-brown with black spots. The butterfly hatches in three to four weeks.

Butterfly:
VI.—VII.
(sometimes also VIII.).
Caterpillar:
Until V.
Foodplants:
Aspen, poplar, usually bushes and smaller trees. Caterpillar hibernates and pupates on the upperside of a leaf.

1 — underside of wings,
2 — caterpillar,
3 — adult

Marsh Fritillary

Euphydryas aurinia ROTTEMBURG, 1775

The range of distribution extends from England through most of Europe as far as Siberia and Korea. A great number of geographical races have arisen in this extensive area. The nominate form comes from the surroundings of Paris. Ssp. *hibernica* Birch. is reported from Ireland, ssp. *scotica* Robs. from Scotland, etc. Most subspecies, however, were named in the eastern part of the palearctic region. A large number of diverse populations live in the vast territories of Siberia and the Far East. The best known Eurasian races include ssp. *davidi* Obth., ssp. *sibirica* Stdgr. and ssp. *lacta* Christ. The species itself is characterized by a marked individual variability, aberrant forms being produced in the same localities in the course of several years. The Marsh Fritillary is normally confined to damp meadows and marshy ground and for this reason its distribution in Europe has an insular character. The drying up of marshy ground has resulted in the disappearance of the butterfly in many places. The female lays light brown, oval-shaped, somewhat flattened eggs, placing them in clusters on the underside of leaves of the foodplant. Initially, the caterpillars share one nest. They pupate in May after hibernation.

Butterfly:
V.—VI.
(in the north and in the mountains also in VII. or even VIII.).
Caterpillar:
From VII. to V.
Foodplants:
Devilsbit scabious, ribwort, plantain.

1 — underside of wings,
2 — caterpillar,
3 — male,
4 — female,
5 — pupa

Spotted Fritillary

Melitaea didyma ESPER, 1777

Lesser Spotted Fritillary

Melitaea trivia SCHIFFERMÜLLER, 1775

The Spotted Fritillary occurs in North Africa, almost all of Europe and central Asia. It is not found in Great Britain, Denmark and the Netherlands. It produces an almost inexhaustible number of forms, both individual and geographical. One would be hard put to find two individuals with completely identical design and colouring. The ground colour of the male is crimson; the colouring of the female varies from different shades of grey to black. The Spotted Fritillary inhabits meadows, woodland clearings and bushy heathland. In some places it is very abundant. The nominate form was described from Bavarian specimens.

The Lesser Spotted Fritillary lives in the south of Europe and penetrates eastwards as far as Iran and Pakistan. The northern boundary of its distribution passes through central Europe where it occurs in Austria and southern Slovakia. It inhabits forest grassland and bushy hillsides. It is only found in warm habitats, where it is quite numerous.

M. didyma:
V.—VI.;
VII.—VIII.
Caterpillar:
From summer to
IV.—V.
Foodplants:
Speedwell,
plantain,
toadflax,
mullein, etc.
It pupates after
hibernation. Stage
of pupa lasts
about two weeks.

M. trivia:
V.—VI., VII.
Foodplants:
Common
mullein.
The development
takes place at
approximately
the same time as
that of the former
species.

M. didyma:
1 — male,
2 — underside of
wings,
3 — female
M. trivia:
4 — underside of
wings,
5 — female

Heath Fritillary

Mellicta athalia ROTTEMBURG, 1775

This is the most widespread and abundant species of the family, occurring in the area extending from the British Isles as far as east Asia, Japan excluded. Its occurrence in England is sporadic, for example in Kent, Essex, Sussex and several habitats in Devon and Cornwall. It is not found in Ireland. The Heath Fritillary inhabits woodland rides, clearings and margins. In the north it penetrates beyond the Arctic Circle and in the Alps it is found at altitudes about 2000 m. Both in the mountains and in the lowlands it is possible to find specimens lacking in pattern, which have the upperside of the wings uniformly dark. The species usually has two generations but only one when living in the mountains. The nominate form, described near Paris, is found in central Europe. Ssp. *biedermanni* Querci and *celadussa* Fruhstorfer live in south-western Europe in Portugal and Spain. Ssp. *norvegica* Aurivillius, described in Dovrefjeld, Norway, is native to Scandinavia. The female lays round, yellow-white eggs on the underside of leaves. The caterpillar is dark with transverse rows of dark spots and yellow-green papillae on the sides. The head is black, speckled yellow. The pupa is grey-white with dark spots.

Butterfly:
V.—VII.;
VIII.—IX.
Caterpillar:
VII.—VI.
Foodplants:
Different species of cow-wheat, plantain, foxglove, etc.

1 — underside of wings,
2 — male,
3 — female,
4 — caterpillar,
5 — pupa

Small Pearl-bordered Fritillary

Clossiana selene SCHIFFERMÜLLER, 1775

Nymphalidae

This species is often common in woodland rides, clearings and shrubby meadows. The ground colour of the upperside of the wings is rusty brown with a black design. It can be distinguished from other fritillaries by the pattern on the underside of the hindwings. Both the pattern and the size are fairly variable. Dark specimens with extended design on the upperside of the wings sometimes appear, both in nature and in captivity. In this case the brown colouring can be seen only along the wing margins in the form of more or less noticeable longitudinal brownish stripes, passing along the veins. The Small Pearl-bordered Fritillary is widespread in the area extending from England as far as Japan and is also reported from North America. It has two generations in central Europe. The summer form is known as gen. aest. *selenia* Fr.; f. *montana* M.D., which occurs at higher elevations in the Alps, has only one generation during the year and is found up to altitudes of about 2000—2400 m. The female lays light green eggs, pointed at the ends, with about 18 longitudinal grooves. Some of the first generation caterpillars grow faster than others, so that they produce another generation of butterflies during the same year. The second generation caterpillars hibernate.

Butterfly:
V.—VII.;
VIII.—IX. (in the north and in the mountains VI.—VIII.).
Caterpillar:
Occurs practically in all months of the year.
Foodplants:
Violet, strawberry, blueberry.

1 — underside of wings,
2 — female,
3 — male,
4 — pupa,
5 — caterpillar

Pearl-bordered Fritillary

Nymphalidae

Clossiana euphrosyne LINNAEUS, 1758

This species is widespread throughout Scandinavia, Great Britain, Ireland and almost all other European countries, being quite abundant in some localities. It penetrates as far east as the regions along Amur and Kamchatka. It inhabits woodland clearings, rides and margins. F. *alpina* Ebert with a more pronounced dark upperside design is native at higher altitudes. Both the ground colour of the wings and the size and intensity of silvery spots on the underside of the hindwings are variable. The female lays cone-shaped eggs, which are at first green and later turn brown. The caterpillar feeds during the summer on dog violet. It is black with a white-blue side stripe. The pupa is grey-brown. In the north as well as in the mountains the species has only one generation. Among the related European species it bears a clear resemblance to the Small Pearl-bordered Fritillary, which is also illustrated in this book. The two species can be distinguished chiefly by the different pattern of the underside of the hindwings, particularly by the distribution and shape of the silvery spots and markings.

Butterfly:
IV.—VII.;
VIII.—IX.
Caterpillar:
V.—IV.
Foodplants:
Common dog violet, strawberry. It hibernates after the second moulting.

1 — female,
2 — male,
3 — underside of wings,
4 — caterpillar,
5 — pupa

Lesser Marbled Fritillary

Brenthis ino ROTTEMBURG, 1775

The species inhabits only marshy meadows, peat-bogs and similar damp localities both in the lowlands and hills, or even quite high up in the mountains. Despite its widely separated locality it is fairly abundant in its habitats. Its distribution area is extensive, comprising northern and western Europe and temperate zone of Asia as far as Japan. It is not found in southern Spain, in Portugal, on islands in the Mediterranean sea or in Greece. The flight of this butterfly is slow, fluttering, close to the ground. It settles on flowers of the thistle, bramble, *Senecio nemorensis* and other plants. There are still many questions concerning the way of life of this Fritillary that remain unexplained. A large number of geographical races occur especially in eastern Asia, and have not yet been fully studied. The female lays light yellow eggs, pointed at the ends, with 14 longitudinal ribs. The caterpillar is light brown with a yellow dorsal band and a dark-edged side one. The spikes are yellowish. The pupa is yellow-brown.

Butterfly:
VI.—VII.
Caterpillar:
From
VII. to VI. of next year.
Foodplants:
Burnet, wood goatsbeard, bramble, etc. It has been proved that both the caterpillar and the egg may hibernate.

1 — male,
2 — female,
3 — underside of wings,
4 — caterpillar

1

3

2

4

Queen of Spain Fritillary

Issoria lathonia LINNAEUS, 1758

The Queen of Spain Fritillary cannot be mistaken for any other species because of the typical large silvery spots on the underside of the hindwings, the size and shape of which are variable. Rarely in nature, but more frequently in captivity, it is possible to find a specimen with these metallic spots forming more or less continuous bands (f. *paradoxa* Fuchs). The upperside of the wings of the f. *valdensis* Esp. is almost completely dark. The Queen of Spain Fritillary is found in fields, meadows and on heathland. In the mountains it ascends as high as 2500 m. It belongs to the group of species which appear from early spring until late autumn. The female lays her eggs singly. The caterpillar is dark grey with a longitudinally split dorsal stripe and a side band, which is sometimes difficult to discern. The pupa is golden-brown with a yellow stripe and shiny metallic spots on the dorsal side. The Queen of Spain Fritillary is a migrant species with its home territory located near the Mediterranean. It also occurs in North Africa, the Canary Islands, Asia Minor and in central Asia and western provinces of China. The species is abundant throughout central Europe. Its migration has been chiefly observed in the Pyrenees. The largest invasions into Britain were recorded in 1872 and 1954.

Butterfly:
In warm regions already from II. or III. (in central Europe from IV. till X.) in 2—3 generations.
Caterpillar:
Throughout the whole year.
Foodplants:
Various species of violet.
The caterpillar hibernates. Pupal stage lasts about 4 weeks.

1 — underside of wings,
2 — male,
3 — female,
4 — caterpillar

1

2

3

4

Dark Green Fritillary

Mesoacidalia aglaja LINNAEUS, 1758

This butterfly inhabits both woodland clearings and meadowland. It has only one generation a year. The butterflies are fond of settling on thistle flowers, sometimes in large numbers. In the mountains, this species is found at considerable elevations up to the forest limit. Very dark females can be found in some places in the mountains (f. *suffusa* Tutt). The nominate form inhabits central Sweden. Ssp. *borealis* Strand, with smaller silvery spots on the underside of the hindwings, lives in the north of Scandinavia. Central European geographical races have been described in central and eastern Asia. In the Himalayas this butterfly is known to occur at altitudes of about 3000 m. Although the Dark Green Fritillary is relatively variable in appearance, it cannot be mistaken for any other species. The underside of the wings is yellowish-green with a pattern of silver spots.

The female lays red-brown eggs with 18 longitudinal ribs, only six of which reach the pole. The caterpillar is black with a white dorsal stripe and red lateral spots. It hibernates in an early stage and reaches maturity the following spring. The pupa is dark with blunt protuberances.

Butterfly:
VI.—VIII.
Caterpillar:
VIII.—V.
Foodplants:
Dog violet, wild pansy and garden pansy. The pupal stage lasts several weeks.

1 — male,
2 — female,
3 — underside of wings

High Brown Fritillary

Nymphalidae

Fabriciana adippe SCHIFFERMÜLLER, 1775

This butterfly is widespread throughout the vast area extending from North Africa over western Europe as far as Japan. It has a large number of geographical races. The nominate form was described near Vienna. Ssp. *bajuvarica* Spul. occurs in German and Austrian Alps, ssp. *norvegica* Schultz breeds in the north of Europe. Many geographical races have been described in eastern Asia, particularly in the extensive regions of China and Japan. Worth a special mention is the f. *cleodoxa* Ochs., which lacks the silvery spots on the underside of hindwings, so that the olive-green or yellow-green colouring with a greenish sheen predominates. In many localities in south-eastern Europe this form is evidently more common than the nominate one. The High Brown Fritillary occurs in habitats similar to those of the related species, mostly in woodland rides and clearings. The butterfly can be well identified by the pattern on the underside of the hindwings. The female lays eggs which are at first greenish and later turn red. The caterpillar is grey-black with rusty-brown spikes. The pupa is brown-grey with blue and silvery spots.

Butterfly:
VI.—VIII.
(sometimes even IX.).
Caterpillar:
In some localities from VIII. to V.; according to other observations the caterpillar hatches as late as in III. feeding until V.—VI. when it pupates.
Foodplants:
Different species of violet.

1 — male,
2 — underside of wings,
3 — f. *cleodoxa* underside of wings,
4 — female

Niobe Fritillary

Fabriciana niobe LINNAEUS, 1758

This species resembles the High Brown Fritillary, but the upperside of its wings is lighter in colour, the tip of the forewing is more rounded and the patches of scent scales are less conspicuous. The silver spots on the underside of the hindwings are smaller, especially those near the base. A darker form of the female, f. *obscura* Spul., also occurs in some localities. The best known individual aberrant form is f. *eris* Meig. It can be found everywhere among the normally coloured individuals, from which it differs by the coloration of the spots on the underside of the hindwings. They are sharply marked, light brown or yellow-brown, but lack the silvery gloss. This form is locally even more abundant than the nominate one. Obviously, an analogy can be seen here to the relationship of the High Brown Fritillary with its form *cleodoxa* Ochs. The Niobe Fritillary inhabits woodland margins and shrubby open country. It is quite abundant in some parts of central Europe. In the Alps it can be found at altitudes of about 2300 to 2550 m. The range of distribution includes all of Europe and Asia Minor; it penetrates eastwards as far as Iran. It is, however, absent in Britain, Corsica, Sardinia and Crete.

Butterfly:
VI.—VIII.
Caterpillar:
leaves the egg shell early in the spring, having hibernated inside the shell. Its development takes place from III. to V. According to other observations the caterpillar hibernates.
Foodplants:
Different species of violet. Pupa stage lasts approximately 4 weeks.

1 — underside of wings,
2 — male,
3 — female
4 — f. *eris* underside of wings

Silver-washed Fritillary

Argynnis paphia LINNAEUS, 1758

The species was described from specimens found in Sweden. In the north of Europe it occurs in central Finland and Sweden and in southern Norway. From there the distribution area extends across Denmark and northwest Germany as far as the Mediterranean. In North Africa it is reported from Algeria. It penetrates eastwards through the extensive regions of Siberia, as far as Japan. In this vast territory it forms a great number of geographical races which are not, as a rule, very sharply separated. The island race, ssp. *immaculata* Bell. from Corsica and Sardinia, is worthy of interest because of the reduced number of silver bands on the underside of the hindwings. Sometimes a dark form of the female, also illustrated here, may occur among the normally coloured individuals. It is well known among collectors as f. *valesina* Esp. The female nearly always lays eggs on the trunks of trees, generally oak, sometimes also on low growing plants near the base of the trunk. The full-grown caterpillar is brownish-black, with a wide yellow dorsal stripe and black and yellow spots on the sides of the body. The pupa is dark brown with yellow dots. The species has only one generation.

Butterfly:
VI.—IX.
Caterpillar:
VIII.—VI.
It pupates after hibernation, usually in V., at higher altitudes in VI.
The period of pupa lasts approximately three weeks.
Foodplants:
Different species of violet, especially common dog violet.

1 — female,
2 — male,
3 — female f. *valesina,*
4 — caterpillar

Cardinal

Nymphalidae

Pandoriana pandora SCHIFFERMÜLLER, 1775

This butterfly can be recognized at first sight by the brick-red or violet colour of the underside of the forewings. The silver bands on the underside of the hindwings are in some individuals very conspicuous, while in others they are so reduced as to almost disappear. The northern boundary of the distribution area of this species passes through central Europe (Austria, southern parts of Czechoslovakia, Hungary). Stray specimens have even been recorded in Poland. In Asia it ascends to altitudes of 3000—4500 m in the mountains. The vast area of its distribution extends from the Canary Islands through North Africa and southern Europe as far as Iran, Afghanistan and Chitral. Up to now, ten individual forms and the same number of geographical races have been described. Ssp. *seitzi* Fruhst. from Algeria and ssp. *pasargades* Fruhst. from central Asia belong to the most outstanding races. During the summer months it flies about waste land, heaths, woodland margins and stony mountain-sides. The egg is brownish-yellow with 20 to 40 longitudinal ribs. The caterpillar is red-brown with a black head. The pupa has shiny spots on its back; the colouring varies from grey-brown to green-grey.

Butterfly:
V.—X.;
in two generations in North Africa:
V.—VI. and VIII.—IX. Single specimens have been observed in X. (also in central Europe).
Caterpillar:
From VII. to V.—VI.
Foodplants:
Violets, particularly pansy.

1 — male,
2 — underside of wings,
3 — caterpillar

Pallas's Fritillary

Argyronome laodice PALLAS, 1771

This butterfly, a swift flier, is found in woodland rides and damp meadows. It is fond of settling on flower plants, especially bramble. Because of the characteristic marking on the underside of the hindwings it is hardly possible to confuse the Pallas's Fritillary with any other species. The outer half of the wing is brown-red or violet, the inner is yellowish. These two parts are separated by a row of shiny white spots that in some cases form a continuous band. The western boundary of its distribution area passes through eastern Europe. Very occasionally it is found in the island of Rügen in the Baltic; it occurs in the northeast regions of Poland, in the Belovezsky Forest and in some parts of the Carpathians. In the Carpathians the species is widespread from east Slovakia as far as Rumania, occurring there only sporadically. A great number of geographical races have been described in the east, particularly in Japan. The caterpillar is grey-black with a yellow dorsal stripe, which is split longitudinally by a black line. It has six dark spots along the sides. The head is reddish-grey. The pupa is shiny dark brown with fine black lines.

Butterfly:
VII.—IX.
Caterpillar:
VIII.—VI.
Foodplants:
Mainly marsh violet and dog violet.

1 — male,
2 — female,
3 — underside of wings,
4 — caterpillar

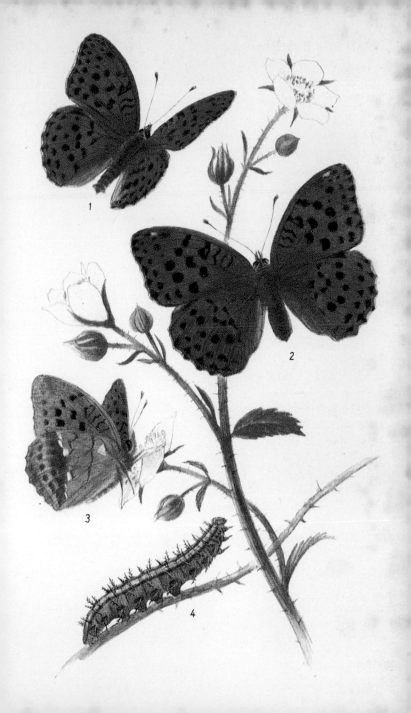

1
2
3
4

Map Butterfly

Araschnia levana LINNAEUS, 1758

This species inhabits woodland rides, parks, edges of meadows and shaded corners overgrown with the stinging nettle. Most often it occurs only sporadically, in some places, however, being very abundant. It can be found throughout the area extending from western Europe as far as Japan, excepting Britain. The Map Butterfly is renowned for its seasonal variability. The ground colour of the wings in the spring specimens (gen. vern. *levana* L.) is brick-red with dark markings. The summer generation specimens (gen. aest. *prorsa* L.) are black with light spots (whitish or yellowish). Occasionally a partial third generation appears but it is difficult to confirm its occurrence in central Europe conclusively, as the development of the caterpillar is very uneven and a possibility of later hatched second generation specimens cannot be excluded. The female lays greenish oval-shaped eggs, attaching them to the underside of leaves joined in columns in a chain-like fashion. At first the caterpillars stay together but later they split up and wander away from each other. When disturbed, they fall off the foodplant onto the ground.

Butterfly:
IV.—V.
(locally also in VI.); VII.—IX.; possibly a 3rd generation even later.
Caterpillar:
VI.—VII.;
VIII.—IX.
Foodplant:
Stinging nettle. Development lasts about 4 weeks.

1 — gen. vern. *levana* (spring form),
2 — caterpillar,
3 — gen. aest. *prorsa* (summer form),
4 — gen. aut. *porima* (autumn form),
5 — gen. vern. *levana* (underside of wings),
6 — pupa

Red Admiral

Vanessa atalanta LINNAEUS, 1758

The Red Admiral is one of the best known of all butterflies. It is found in the Azores and Canary Islands, in North Africa, and throughout the whole of Europe as far as Asia Minor and Iran. It is native in North America and penetrates as far south as Guatemala. It has been discovered in Haiti and New Zealand, but it is probable that it was introduced there. There are no outstanding geographical races even in this extensive area as the Red Admiral is a migrant species. Up-to-date observations done in central Europe indicate that even there, where this species is very abundant, immigration of large numbers of the Red Admiral takes place. Cases of successful hibernation of the species have been recorded in central Europe but, nevertheless, the immigrant specimens are most important for the preservation of the population. Their offspring can be seen along the woodland margins in gardens, orchards and parks. The Red Admiral is fond of settling on the trunks of fruit-trees in late summer, sucking the over-ripe windfalls, particularly pears and plums. It often ascends high up in the mountains, where it rests on flowering plants along the streams.

Butterfly:
V.—X.
Caterpillar:
Individually from V. to IX., sometimes also in X. Butterflies reach western and central Europe in V. as a rule.
Foodplant:
Stinging nettle.

1 — underside of wings,
2 — adult,
3 — caterpillar,
4 — pupa

Painted Lady

Nymphalidae

Vanessa cardui LINNAEUS, 1758

The Painted Lady inhabits fields, heaths, steppes and meadows, avoiding forests. It is one of the best known migrant butterflies, arriving in central and western Europe from the south, usually in June. The migration of this species has been observed high up in the mountains. There are many detailed records concerning the immigration of the Painted Lady in English literature. A large invasion of the species was recorded in 1948; also in 1952, the species being conspicuously abundant in western and northern Europe. The geographical distribution of the Painted Lady covers an extensive area. It occurs almost universally throughout the world, the exception being South America. It is one of the few butterflies found in Iceland and Ireland. The female lays single eggs on leaves of the foodplant of the caterpillar. The caterpillar is spiny, grey or brownish with yellow stripes. The pupa is greyish or brown, with shiny golden spots. The butterfly hatches in about two weeks.

Butterfly:
Arriving from the south coast from IV.—VI., next generation until X.
Caterpillar:
VI.—IX.
Foodplants:
Different plants, chiefly thistle, burdock, stinging nettle, etc. It may be a pest on globe artichokes in the south.

1 — underside of wings,
2 — adult,
3 — pupa,
4 — caterpillar

Camberwell Beauty

Nymphalis antiopa LINNAEUS, 1758

The Camberwell Beauty enjoys much attention from the collectors because of its suitability for experiments concerning the influence of temperature on the wing pattern. The well-known f. *hygiaea* Heydenr. is illustrated here. It occurs in deciduous forests both in the lowlands and quite high up in the mountains, and prefers river-sides, streams and river banks with abundance of the caterpillar's foodplants. With the first sunny spring days the Camberwell Beauty leaves the sheltered places where it hibernated. It is fond of sucking sap oozing from injured trees or the sweet juice from over-ripe fruits. This large butterfly inhabits Europe, Asia and North America but does not breed in England or Ireland. The nominate form was described from specimens captured in Sweden. It occurs in central and western Europe and is common in parts of North America, where two other geographical races are found (ssp. *hyperborea* Seitz and ssp. *lintnerii* Fitsch). Further subspecies have been described in east Asia. The butterfly is still abundant in some places but it seems to have decreased in number during the last few decades.

Butterfly:
VI.—IX. and after hibernation from III. or IV. to V., the mountain specimens to VI.
Caterpillar:
VI.—VII.
Foodplants:
Willow, sallow, birch, poplar, elm.

1 — adult,
2 — caterpillar,
3 — f. *hygiaea*,
4 — pupa

Large Tortoiseshell

Nymphalis polychloros LINNAEUS, 1758

The Large Tortoiseshell lives in woods, parks, avenues and cemeteries. In the same way as the Camberwell Beauty, it likes to suck sap leaking from injured trunks of birch, oak and fruit trees. The species used to be much more plentiful, the caterpillars in some places even causing damage, but during the last decades it has been getting rare. It is widespread from North Africa across the whole of Europe (except Ireland) and Asia Minor as far as the Himalayas. Ssp. *erythromelas* Aust. inhabits the mountains of North Africa. The best known individual forms are those produced by the effect of high and low temperatures on the chrysalides. The illustrated f. *testudo* Esp. is one of them. It is distinguished from the representative form by the conspicuously different pattern of the wings. The female lays her eggs after hibernation. They are red-brown and barrel-shaped. The caterpillars live gregariously and disperse only before pupating. The pupal stage lasts two to three weeks. In many places the Large Tortoiseshell lives together with the Camberwell Beauty, having a similar way of life and seasonal habits.

Butterfly:
VI.—IX. and after hibernation from III. to V.
Caterpillar:
V.—VII.
Foodplants:
Sallow, willow, elm, wych elm, poplar and fruit trees.

1 — caterpillar,
2 — adult,
3 — pupa,
4 — f. *testudo*

False Comma

Nymphalis vau-album SCHIFFERMÜLLER, 1775

The question of systematic classification of this species still remains in dispute; sometimes it is classified as a member of the *Nymphalis* Kluk genus, sometimes it is considered to belong to the *Polygonia* Hb. genus. Nor is the nomenclature constant: in older literature the species is called *l-album* Esper, but this name is younger than the denomination *vau-album*, used by Schiffermüller. The western boundary of its distribution passes through central Europe from where it is widespread as far as Japan. It is a regular species in Rumania and Bulgaria; in Czechoslovakia it is very rare. Isolated specimens have been reported from southern Finland and Sweden. The species forms numerous geographical races in east Asia. It is found in North America and in southern parts of Canada. The female lays eggs on the twigs of trees on which the caterpillar feeds. The eggs are greenish and barrel-shaped. The caterpillars live gregariously at first in finely spun webs. The pupa is grey-brown with four silver spots. The butterfly inhabits deciduous forests and groves, and is quite shy.

Butterfly: VII.—IX. and after hibernation to IV. or V.
Caterpillar: V.—VII.
Foodplants: Elm, aspen, different species of willow, birch, etc.

1 — adult,
2 — caterpillar,
3 — underside of wings

Peacock Butterfly

Inachis io LINNAEUS, 1758

Owing to its interesting wing design, the Peacock Butterfly is so conspicuous that it cannot be mistaken for any other species. It occurs throughout most of Europe and the temperate part of Asia including Japan. Only a few geographical forms are recognized in this extensive area. Like other related species, the Peacock Butterfly is able to produce different forms if the fresh pupa is subjected to sudden changes in temperature. The butterfly is almost everywhere; it can be found in lowland forests, parks, gardens and high up in the mountains where it likes to settle on flowering plants, particularly thistles. It hibernates in lofts, cellars, caves and similar sheltered places and leaves them in early spring. The Peacock and the Small Tortoiseshell feeding from the catkins of a sallow bush are a characteristic feature of spring. The female lays eggs in batches on the undersides of leaves of the caterpillar's foodplants. The young caterpillars crawl to the top of the plant where they spin a communal nest. They live gregariously. The pupa has two forms, grey or yellowish-green.

Butterfly:
VII.—IX., after hibernation from III. to V., in the mountains also in VI.
Caterpillar:
From V. to VI. and then from VII. to IX. The egg stage lasts about a week; caterpillar 2—3 weeks; pupa 10—14 days.
Foodplants:
Almost exclusively on stinging nettle, rarely on hop.

1 — underside of wings,
2 — adult,
3 — pupa,
4 — caterpillar

Small Tortoiseshell

Aglais urticae LINNAEUS, 1758

This butterfly is found in nature during almost all seasons of the year. The Small Tortoiseshell — like the Peacock Butterfly — hibernates in caves, cellars, lofts and outbuildings. It is on the wing from March onwards and can be seen even in the parks of big cities. Throughout the whole of Europe, the Small Tortoiseshell is one of the most common species of butterfly. It inhabits gardens, fields and woodland margins, not only in the lowlands, but also high up in the mountains. It appears at altitudes of about 3000 m in the Alps, and up to 5000 m in the Himalayas. High mountain races, ssp. *ladakensis* Moore and ssp. *rizana* Moore, deserve special mention. Some authors consider the two of them to be independent species, similarly to Corsican ssp. *ichnusa* Hb. In the nearctic region the Small Tortoiseshell is replaced by the similar species *Aglais milberti* God. The Small Tortoiseshell inhabits the vast area extending from the British Isles as far as Japan. The distribution of the species is almost continuous in Europe, from the south up to the arctic region, where the ssp. *polaris* Stdgr. has been described.

Butterfly:
VI.—IX., sometimes also X. and after hibernation from III. to V.
Caterpillar:
V.—VIII.
The chrysalis stage lasts about two weeks.
Foodplant:
Stinging nettle.

1 — adult,
2 — caterpillar,
3 — f. *ichnusoides* Sel.,
4 — underside of wings,
5 — pupa

Comma Butterfly

Polygonia c-album LINNAEUS, 1758

The Comma Butterfly has a small white spot, resembling by its shape "C" on the underside of the hindwings. Many separate forms have been described, the distinctive element being the shape of this spot, which is very changeable. These forms have little taxonomic significance, but for interest's sake, some of them should be mentioned: *o-album* Newh., *delta-album* Der., *j-album* Spul., *f-album* Esp., *g-album* Gillm., etc. However, the specimens lacking this spot did not escape the attention of collectors and they can be found in many collections under names *c-extinctum* Schultz or *extincta* Rbl. The Comma Butterfly hibernates, the hibernating specimens being only those of the typical form. The specimens hatching in summer are partly typical, partly much lighter in colour (f. *hutchinsoni* Robs.). The butterflies of the typical form hibernate, while the light specimens breed again; their offspring, which appear in August or September of the same year, are typical and hibernate. Consequently, it is only typically coloured specimens that appear in spring, never the f. *hutchinsoni* Robs. The distribution area of the Comma Butterfly extends from the British Isles as far as Japan.

Butterfly:
VI.—VII.;
VII.—V. or
VIII.—V.
Caterpillar:
V.—VII.,
but also in
VII.—VIII.
Foodplant:
Stinging nettle,
hop, elm,
gooseberry,
currant, etc.

1 — adult,
2 — pupa,
3 — underside of
wings,
4 — caterpillar,
5 — f. *hutchinsoni*

Speckled Wood

Pararge aegeria LINNAEUS, 1758

The Speckled Wood is an inconspicuous brown butterfly inhabiting woodland rides, clearings, parks, etc. It can also be found fluttering along the less frequented country lanes. Its flight is slow, hesitant, and it often settles on low branches or even on the ground. Its distribution area is quite extensive, from western Europe and North Africa as far as central Asia. In the Alps it ascends to altitudes of about 1500 m, in African mountains even higher. There are a considerable number of geographical races. The nominate form was described in southern Europe. The spots on the wings are orange, in contrast to those of the specimens from central Europe which are yellowish. The nominate form lives in southern Europe and North Africa (Morocco, Algeria, Tunisia). Ssp. *tircis* Butler is reported from Britain and Ireland. Ssp. *insula* How. was described in St. Mary's Island (Scilly Isles) in 1971. The west-European populations known as ssp. *tircis* Butler, 1867, and the central-European ones known as ssp. *egerides* Staudinger, 1871, are considered by some authors to be identical.

Butterfly:
III.—VI.;
VII.—IX.,
sometimes also X.
Caterpillar:
VI.—VII. and from IX. to the next year's spring. The butterfly breeds continuously through the summer and hibernation takes place either in the caterpillar or pupal stage.
Foodplants:
Couch grass, meadow grass, etc.

1 — male,
2 — male ssp. *tircis,*
3 — female ssp. *tircis,*
4 — caterpillar

Wall Brown
Lasiommata megera LINNAEUS, 1767

Large Wall Brown
Lasiommata maera LINNAEUS, 1758

The Wall Brown is widespread from North Africa and western Europe to Asia Minor and Iran; it occurs also in Great Britain and Ireland. It inhabits mostly fields, but also forest margins, gardens, moorland and city parks. It settles on stones, fences and walls. The eggs of this species are light green and oval with a net-like surface structure. The caterpillar is green, with whitish lines. The Wall Brown has two generations in most areas, except for the south, where three generations may appear.

The Large Wall Brown is also found in North Africa and western Europe, but it penetrates further eastward to central Asia and the Himalayas. In the north it occurs in the arctic region of Norway. The species shows a considerable geographical variability. The central European populations are classified as the nominate form, which was originally described according to material from Sweden. Ssp. *orientalpina* Verity lives in the southern valleys of the Alps; ssp. *meadewaldoi* Rothsch. from Algeria is another interesting race. The strong variability of this species is appreciated when a large series collected in the same habitat in different years can be compared. There are two generations during the year except in the north and the mountain regions, where only one generation appears.

L. megera:
IV.—X.
Caterpillar:
Almost
all the year round.
Foodplants:
Meadow grass,
cocksfoot grass,
etc.

L. maera:
V.—VI.,
VIII.—IX.
Caterpillar:
From VI. to VII.
and from autumn
to V.
Foodplants:
Various grasses,
particularly
meadow grass
and floating
sweet grass.

L. megera:
1 — male
L. maera:
2 — male,
3 — female,
4 — caterpillar,
5 — pupa

Marbled White

Melanargia galathea LINNAEUS, 1758

It is impossible to mistake this species for any other butterfly in central Europe. There are, however, several similar species in southern Europe, Asia Minor and North Africa. The distribution area extends from western Europe as far as Iran and North Africa. It is found at altitudes of about 1700 m in the mountains and in the Atlas mountains even higher. The butterfly inhabits woodland clearings, rides and margins, railway banks and grassy hillsides, in some places being very abundant. It likes to settle on flowers of the field scabious. The female is larger than the male. It lays its eggs loosely, so that they fall off the grass or often even releases them while in flight. The caterpillar feeds only at night, remaining hidden during the daytime. The marbled white is very variable, both individually and geographically, and so it is not surprising that many subspecies have been described. The nominate form lives in central Europe; ssp. *lucasi* Ramb. is the form found in North Africa. F. *procida* Herbst with a reduced pale wing pattern is one of the more conspicuous individual forms. It occurs in different types of habitat, being most abundant in the south.

Butterfly:
VI.—VIII.
Caterpillar:
From summer to
V.—VI.
Foodplants:
Timothy grass, meadow grass, cocksfoot grass, and other species of grass.

1 — male,
2 — female,
3 — caterpillar
4 — male (yellow form)

Grayling

Hipparchia semele LINNAEUS, 1758

The incidence and way of life of this butterfly are very interesting. It is found not only in forests and parks but also on heaths, both with stony and sandy soil. It ascends from sea level to a height of about 1700 m. It rests with folded wings on the ground or on tree trunks and so easily escapes notice. The butterfly feeds on flower nectar, especially on wild thyme, but is also attracted by injured trees with leaking sap. Its flight is rapid, but only for short distances. The distribution area is considerable; it extends from Ireland and Great Britain across the whole of Europe as far as Asia Minor and Transcaucasia. In Ireland, as late as 1971, ssp. *hibernica* How. was differentiated from the already known ssp. *clarencis* de Lattin. Ssp. *anglorum* Verity is native to England. The nominate form was described according to the material from Sweden. Several species bearing very close resemblance, and fairly difficult to distinguish, live in the southern part of the distribution area. The caterpillar is light yellow with darker stripes. The pupa is rounded and plump, golden brown in colour and lies buried just under the surface of the ground in a silk-lined cocoon.

Butterfly: VI.—IX.
Caterpillar: From summer to V. of the next year.
Foodplants: Different species of grass, e.g. tussock grass, sheep's fescue, etc.

1 — male,
2 — female,
3 — underside of wings,
4 — caterpillar

Hermit

Chazara briseis LINNAEUS, 1764

This is a late summer butterfly of central Europe. In the south, however, it is found already in June. It inhabits dry localities, stony hillsides, woodland margins, fields, railway tracks, etc. It flies rapidly and is quite shy. The butterfly settles with folded wings, the colouring of which ' — especially the underside — makes it difficult to distinguish the individual from the background. The Hermit is one of the most geographically variable butterflies, the different races being distinguished by the width and intensity of the white band on the wings. The caterpillar is yellow-grey, striped and thick. The pupa has a dark dorsal band. The species was described from German specimens. Ssp. *bataia* Fruhst., which differs from other races mainly by a reduction of pale markings, especially in the male, lives in Bohemia. Farther south, the width of the band increases, especially on the hindwings, and the wing-span becomes larger. In f. *pirata* Esp. the white colour of the bands is replaced by orange-brown.

The Hermit is widespread from western Europe as far as the Pamir and the Altai. It is also known to occur in North Africa.

Butterfly:
VI.—IX.
Caterpillar:
From summer to V.—VI. The egg stage lasts about two weeks.
Foodplants:
Different species of grass, mainly blue moor grass.

1 — underside of wings,
2 — caterpillar,
3 — male,
4 — female

Great Banded Grayling

Satyridae

Brintesia circe FABRICIUS, 1775

The Great Banded Grayling is quite unmistakable. From the late spring to high summer it can be found in forests, particularly in those with a preponderance of oak trees, where it likes to settle on the thick trunks. When disturbed it starts off immediately and flies quite a long distance before it settles again. It inhabits the regions near the Mediterranean, penetrating northwards to central Europe and eastwards as far as Iran and even the Himalayas. The occurrence of this species tends to be discontinuous along the northern boundary of its distribution area, although the butterfly is fairly common in some localities. It is absent in northern and north-western Europe, in North Africa and Great Britain. Only a few well-defined geographical races have been described so far. The female differs from the male by greater size; she also has a wider white band on the wings. The caterpillar searches for food only at night, staying hidden in the daytime. It is red-brown, with longitudinal lines, and has an ochre-yellow, white-bordered band above the legs; the head is light brown with black lines. The pupa is chestnut-brown with yellow spots.

Butterfly:
VI.—VII., in some places until IX.
Caterpillar:
From summer to VI.
Foodplants:
Different species of grass, e.g. rye-grass, brome grass, etc.

1 — caterpillar,
2 — underside of wings,
3 — female

Woodland Grayling

Hipparchia fagi SCOPOLI, 1763

The distribution area of this south-European species extends to central Europe. It does not live in Portugal, Great Britain or in northern Europe. Although the species is usually rather local it is not uncommon to find it in abundance in some regions. It inhabits woods and grassy clearings, sometimes together with the Great Banded Grayling. In the same way as the latter, the Woodland Grayling rests on tree trunks and when disturbed flies off immediately. It resembles especially the Rock Grayling (*Hipparchia alcyone* Schiffermüller), which is smaller and has a brownish edge, wider than the adjoining white band on the upperside of hindwings. This edging is narrower in the Woodland Grayling. Also the design of the underside of the wings, particularly the hindwings, shows certain differences. In the female the wings have a fairly wide, lighter band. The females of the Woodland Grayling, like those of the Great Banded Grayling, are rarer than the males. The caterpillar is red-grey and striped. It stays hidden during the daytime, venturing out at night in search of food. The head is light, with four black bars. The pupa is dark brown.

Butterfly:
VI.—VIII.
Caterpillar:
After hibernation
to V.—VI.
Foodplants:
Different species
of soft grass.

1 — male,
2 — caterpillar,
3 — female

Meadow Brown

Satyridae

Maniola jurtina LINNAEUS, 1758

The species is widespread in the area extending from the Canary Islands and North Africa across the whole of Europe as far as Asia Minor and Iran. In some regions it is very abundant. It is one of the most common butterflies in central Europe. The Meadow Brown occurs almost everywhere: in meadows, fields, woodland margins, clearings, ditches. It is even found in city parks and cemeteries. The male is easily distinguished from the female by the presence of an orange patch on the forewings and larger eye-spots. Different races appear in the periphery of the distribution area; ssp. *iernes* Graves, described in Ireland; ssp. *splendida* White from the Lunga Islands and West Scotland, etc. Ssp. *hispulla* Esp., common in the south (Canary Islands, North Africa, islands of the Mediterranean including Malta, Spain, Portugal) is very well known. Its orange pattern on the upperside of the wings is more intense. The female lays eggs singly on grasses. The eggs are at first yellow, latter become mottled with red-brown. The caterpillar hatches in about 25 days. It is in two shades of green, striped, and covered with fine grey hair.

Butterfly:
VI.—VIII., in some places also IX.
Caterpillar:
From summer to V. of the next year. It hibernates after the second moulting.
Foodplants:
Various grasses, especially meadow grass.

1 — underside of wings (male),
2 — male,
3 — female,
4 — caterpillar

Dusky Meadow Brown

Hyponephele lycaon KÜHN, 1774

The male bears a resemblance to the Meadow
Brown. However, it differs conspicuously from it
by the design on the underside of the hindwings
and also in some other respects as is shown in the
illustration. The females of the two species can
be recognized at first sight by the two spots in the
brown-orange patch on the forewings. Related
species, the Oriental Meadow Brown (*Hyponephele
lupina* Costa, 1836), lives in southern Europe. The
distribution range of the Dusky Meadow Brown
in Europe is rather local. It is not found in the
British Isles, Scandinavia, North Africa, Denmark,
Holland or Belgium, but it does occur in central
Europe, where it is quite common particularly in
the southern part. The Dusky Meadow Brown
inhabits dry places, mainly fallow land, stony
hillsides and railway tracks. It flies slowly, low
above the ground, often settling on flowers of
the scabious and other plants. The female lays her
eggs singly. Initially they are white, later pinkish.
The caterpillar hatches in about four weeks. It
searches for food at night, staying hidden in the
daytime. Its double dorsal line, brightly coloured
head, and red spikes around the anus are characteristic. The pupa is red-brown with white stripes.

Butterfly:
VI.—VIII.
Caterpillar:
From summer to
V. of the next
year.
Foodplants:
Different grasses,
especially
meadow grass.

1 — caterpillar,
2 — male,
3 — female,
4 — underside of
wings (male),
5 — pupa

Dryad

Satyridae

Minois dryas SCOPOLI, 1763

The distribution area of the Dryad is considerable, spreading from northern Spain across the whole of Europe and the temperate zone of Asia as far as Japan. The species tends to have a predilection for certain localities, and so its occurrence, especially in Europe, is in isolated patches. It is not, therefore, surprising that this kind of geographical isolation has resulted in the creation of many geographical races. The species does not live in southern Spain, southern Italy, Greece, the Mediterranean islands, or in the north of the Continent. It does not occur in Great Britain, either. In the Alps it is found at altitudes of about 1500 m. The Dryad inhabits dry shrubby regions, woodland margins and clearings. It flies slowly and clumsily, low above the ground, never leaving the confines of its habitat. In its central European habitats it can hardly be mistaken for any other species. The female does not fix her eggs but drops them near the foodplant. The egg is at first yellow, later turns brownish, and then, shortly before the caterpillar hatches, greyish. It hatches in about 34 days. The caterpillar hibernates after the second moult. It is greyish-yellow with dark stripes. The pupa is brown.

Butterfly:
VII.—VIII., sometimes also IX.
Caterpillar:
From IX. to V.—VI. The pupal stage lasts about four weeks.
Foodplants:
Various grasses, e.g. oat grass, brome grass, cocksfoot grass, meadow grass, sheep's fescue, etc.

1 — female,
2 — caterpillar,
3 — male

Small Heath
Coenonympha pamphilus LINNAEUS, 1758

Pearly Heath
Coenonympha arcania LINNAEUS, 1761

Chestnut Heath
Coenonympha glycerion BORKHAUSEN, 1788

A number of similar species are included in the *Coenonympha* Hb. genus. They are small, inconspicuously coloured butterflies. The three most common European species are illustrated here.

The Small Heath lives almost everywhere. It is found in ditches along roads, in unused building plots in centres of big cities, etc. It occurs in all European countries including England and Ireland. Its flight is slow and fluttering. It settles on flowers and grass stalks. The Small Heath hibernates in different stages of development.

The Pearly Heath inhabits woodland clearings and meadows, in some places being quite abundant. It is not found in England, Ireland, nor in some of the islands in the Mediterranean.

The Chestnut Heat flies about woodland clearings and meadows. It is widespread in the area extending from western Europe to east Asia, but does not occur in Scandinavia, Britain, Ireland, Belgium, the Netherlands, or Portugal.

C. pamphilus:
IV.—X. in several generations.
Caterpillar:
From summer to spring.
Foodplants:
Meadow grass, crested dogtail etc.

C. arcania:
V.—IX. in one or two generations.
Caterpillar:
From summer to V.
Foodplants:
Melick grass.

C. glycerion:
VI.—VIII.
Caterpillar:
Until V.
Foodplants:
Crested dogtail, false brome grass, melick, etc.

C. pamphilus:
1 — underside of wings,
4 — male,
7 — caterpillar,
9 — pupa
C. glycerion:
2 — male,
3 — female,
5 — underside of wings
C. arcania:
6 — underside of wings,
8 — female

Woodland Ringlet

Erebia medusa SCHIFFERMÜLLER, 1775

Scotch Argus
Erebia aethiops ESPER, 1777

The Woodland Ringlet is one of the most wide-spread European species of the *Erebia* Dalm. genus. It occurs both in the lowlands and in the hills and even quite high up in the mountains. In the Alps it is found at altitudes of about 2600 m; in the Carpathians 1600—1900 m. The species was first described near Vienna, Austria. It forms several important geographical races, e.g. ssp. *hippomedusa* Ochsenheimer, 1820, found at higher elevations in the Austrian and Italian Alps. The butterflies inhabit mainly damp meadows.

The Scotch Argus prefers hilly regions, and is often found in the mountains. At higher altitudes (1700—2000 m) smaller specimens occur with much reduced red-brown pattern. (f. *altivaga* Fruhst.). The distribution range extends from western Europe as far as east Asia. It is absent from Scandinavia. The caterpillar stays in concealed places. The pupa is brownish-yellow and wrapped in a lightly spun cocoon.

E. medusa:
V.—VI., in the mountains to VII.
Caterpillar:
From summer to spring.
Foodplants:
Hairy finger-grass.

E. aethiops:
VII.—IX.
Caterpillar:
From IX. to VI.
Foodplants:
Meadow grass, bennet, cocksfoot grass, etc.

E. medusa:
1 — adult,
2 — caterpillar,
3 — underside of wings,
5 — pupa,
E. aethiops:
4 — adult

Large Ringlet

Erebia euryale ESPER, 1805

Arran Brown

Erebia ligea LINNAEUS, 1758

The specimens from the Riesengebirge mountains in Bohemia were used for the original description of the Large Ringlet. The species is found in mountainous localities in the area extending from the Pyrenees to the Ural and the Altai. Like many other members of the genus, the Large Ringlet is a very variable species. It inhabits mountain meadows and woodland rides. It is fond of resting on flowers of the snakeweed and ragwort. The Large Ringlet is very abundant in some years. The caterpillar takes two years to reach its full development.

The Arran Brown was first described in Sweden. It favours hilly country and lower altitudes in the mountains. It seldom ascends higher than 1500 m in Europe. The distribution area ranges from western Europe to Japan. The female lays oval yellowish eggs. The caterpillars either hatch in a few weeks after the eggs have been laid or do not leave the protective egg shell until the next spring. Only some of the caterpillars pupate, the imago emerging in the same year. Most of the almost full-grown caterpillars hibernate again. The brown pupa with a dark pattern lies loose on the ground.

The two species look alike but they are distinguishable, particularly by the design on the underside of the hindwings.

E. euryale:
VII.—VIII.
Caterpillar:
Period of two years.
Foodplants:
Different grasses, e.g. wood millet, finger-grass, sheep's fescue, etc. It pupates in VI.

E. ligea:
VI.—VIII.
Caterpillar:
Until V.
Foodplants:
Wood millet, finger-grass, etc.

E. euryale:
1 — adult,
2 — underside of wings,
E. ligea:
3 — caterpillar,
4 — adult,
5 — underside of wings,
6 — pupa

Purple Hairstreak

Quercusia quercus LINNAEUS, 1758

Brown Hairstreak

Thecla betulae LINNAEUS, 1758

The Purple Hairstreak is an inhabitant of oak forests. It is difficult to see in high woods because it stays, as a rule, round the tops of trees, fluttering about and settling from time to time on the leaves. The distribution area extends from North Africa and western Europe including England and southern Ireland to Asia Minor and Trans-caucasia. The female has a shiny violet patch on the upperside of the forewings, while the male has an overall purplish sheen on a grey-black ground colour. The red-brown caterpillar has yellow or red dots along the black dorsal stripe. The pupa is brown, with dark spots and dots. The pupal stage lasts about 2 weeks.

The Brown Hairstreak lives in deciduous forests, parks and town cemeteries. In the mountains it is not found at altitudes higher than 1000 m. It is widespread in the area extending from western Europe, including England and Ireland, as far as Mongolia, China and Korea. It is never numerous in its habitats and usually only single specimens can be found. The female has a large rich orange patch on the forewings. The characteristic coloration of the underside of the wings also simplifies the identification of the Brown Hairstreak. The green caterpillar has a brown head and a double yellow dorsal stripe. The pupa is brown with yellow markings. The pupal stage lasts 15 to 21 days.

Q. quercus:
VI.—VIII.
Caterpillar:
IV.—VI.
Foodplant:
Oak.
The egg
hibernates.

T. betulae:
VII.—X.
Caterpillar:
V.—VI.
Foodplants:
Blackthorn, birch,
etc. The egg
hibernates.

Q. quercus:
1 — male,
2 — female,
3 — underside of
wings
T. betulae:
4 — female

White-letter Hairstreak
Strymonidia w-album KNOCH, 1782

Green Hairstreak
Callophrys rubi LINNAEUS, 1758

The White-letter Hairstreak has a white broken band on the underside of the hindwings, resembling in shape the letter "W". Single specimens inhabit woodland rides and the shrubby margins of deciduous forests, where they like to bask in sunny places. The species is never found in large numbers. It is widespread in the area stretching from western Europe, including southern England, to Japan. The green caterpillar has white protuberances on the back. The head is light brown; the abdomen is green, with red spots. The pupa is grey-brown and this stage lasts 15 to 21 days.

The upperside of the wings of the Green Hairstreak is brown, contrasting with the beautifully grass-green underside. It lives on shrubby hillsides, along the margins of woodlands and in clearings. In the Alps it is found at altitudes of about 1800 m. It occurs in North Africa, throughout most of Europe and the temperate zone of Asia as far as Åmur. It also extends far to the north, where ssp. *borealis* Krul. has been described. The underside of the wings of this subspecies is greenish-yellow, as opposed to the bright green of the nominate form. The green caterpillar has a dark-edged yellow dorsal band and light side stripes. The pupa is brown, with light spiracles.

S. w-album:
VI.—VIII.
Caterpillar:
V.—VI.
Foodplants:
Wych elm, elm.
The egg
hibernates.

C. rubi: III.—VI.,
Partial second
generation in the
south.
Caterpillar:
V.—VIII.
Foodplants:
Seeds
of broom and
dogwood,
bilberry etc.
The pupa
hibernates.

C. rubi:
1 — male,
4 — underside of
wings
S. w-album:
2 — male,
3 — underside of
wings

Scarce Copper

Heodes virgaureae LINNAEUS, 1758

Large Copper

Lycaena dispar HAWORTH, 1803

The Scarce Copper is characterized by the conspicuous sexual dimorphism, i.e. the different pattern of the male and female. It inhabits thin woodland, clearings and meadows. It flies rapidly, often settling on flowers. It is widespread throughout the north of Europe to Transcaucasia and Mongolia. It is missing from England. In the mountains it rises to altitudes of about 2000 m. The dark green caterpillar has a black head and yellow stripes and protuberances. The pupa is brown.

H. virgaureae:
VI.—VIII.;
in some localities
even IX.
Caterpillar:
IV.—VI.
Foodplant:
Dock

The Large Copper is a very variable species. The first specimens were described in England where, however, it became extinct in the middle of the 19th century. A number of these English specimens can be found in private collections and in the larger museums, and are considered to be exceptionally valuable. Ssp. *batava* Obth. from the Netherlands (Friesland) bears the closest resemblance to the nominate form. A number of further races have been described in France and other European countries. The illustrated ssp. *rutila* Werneburg, 1864 occurs in the south-eastern parts of central Europe. It lives in marshy meadows, especially in regions subject to flooding, sometimes visiting dry fields with flowering clover or lucerne. The dark green caterpillar has a brown head and light side stripes. The pupa is grey, with brown markings. The rate of development of the caterpillars fluctuates considerably so that pupation may take place within 14 days or as long as several months.

L. dispar:
V.—VI.;
VII.—VIII.
Caterpillar:
From
summer to V.
Foodplants:
Different species
of dock,
particularly
water dock.

H. virgaureae:
1 — female,
2 — male,
4 — underside of
wings
L. dispar:
3 — male,
5 — underside of
wings,
6 — female

Purple-edged Copper

Palaeochrysophanus hippothoë LINNAEUS, 1761

Purple-shot Copper

Heodes alciphron ROTTEMBURG, 1775

The Purple-edged Copper inhabits damp meadows and sub-alpine pastures. It is fairly abundant most years. The butterflies usually rest on flowers of the knotgrass. The species is widely distributed and scattered because its breeding localities are restricted. It occurs in the area extending from western Europe to east Asia. The mountain ssp. *eurydame* Hoffmannsegg lives at high altitudes in the Alps (approximately up to 2300 m). Ssp. *stiberi* Gerh. was described from the north of Scandinavia. The dark green caterpillar has light notches between the segments. The head is brown, the side stripes light. The dark yellow pupa is dotted with black.

The Purple-shot Copper is fond of localities similar to those favoured by the former butterfly. It likes to settle on flowering bramble or thyme. A remarkable race, with reduced violet sheen, lives in the south of Europe; the illustrated south-European specimen was captured in Spain. The species is widespread throughout Europe and eastwards as far as Iran. The faint green caterpillar has a brown head and two dorsal and two side stripes. The bulky pupa is grey with a green tint and brown dots.

P. hippothoë:
V.—VIII.
Caterpillar:
From summer to V.
Foodplants:
Knotgrass and dock.

H. alciphron:
VI.—VIII.
Caterpillar:
From summer to V.
Foodplant:
Dock.

P. hippothoë:
1 — male,
2 — female,
H. alciphron:
3 — male,
4 — ssp.
gordius (male)

1

2

3

4

Small Copper

Lycaena phlaeas LINNAEUS, 1761

Violet Copper
Lycaena helle SCHIFFERMÜLLER, 1775

Sooty Copper
Heodes tityrus PODA, 1761

The Small Copper is one of the most common butterflies. It is widespread throughout the whole of Europe and the temperate zone of Asia including Japan. It also occurs in the eastern parts of the U.S.A., in Canada and in Ethiopia. The habitats of this species are very varied: Meadows, fields, gardens, hillsides, etc. From spring to autumn, two or more generations appear; in the south (e.g. the Canary Islands) the imago is present all the year round. The caterpillar, too, passes through different phases of development throughout the year.

The Violet Copper lives in central and northern Europe, penetrating eastwards as far as Siberia. It inhabits only wet meadows. One or two generations appear from May to October. It has become extinct in many places in central Europe as its favourite habitats are being continually drained.

The Sooty Copper inhabits meadows, fields and clearings. It is quite abundant in some places. Ssp. *subalpinus* Speyer is found at altitudes of about 2000 m in the Alps. The distribution range of the Sooty Copper extends from Europe to the temperate zone of Asia. It is not found in Scandinavia, Finland and southern Spain, nor in Great Britain. Ssp. *bleusei* Obth. occurs in central Spain.

L. phlaeas:
Caterpillar:
V.—VI.,
VI.—VIII.,
X.—IV.
Foodplants:
Dock and sorrel.

L. helle:
Caterpillar:
V.—VI. and
VIII.—IX.
Foodplant:
Knotgrass.

H. tityrus:
IV.—V.,
VII.—VIII.,
partial third
generation in the
south.
Caterpillar:
VI.—VII. and
from autumn
to IV.
Foodplant: Dock.

L. helle:
1 — male,
L. phlaeas:
2 — male,
3 — f.
coeruleopunctata
(female)
H. tityrus:
4 — male,
5 — female

Adonis Blue

Lysandra bellargus ROTTEMBURG, 1775

Chalk-hill Blue

Lysandra coridon PODA, 1761

The Adonis Blue inhabits uncultivated fields, railway banks, dry hillsides and downland. It is distributed throughout Europe and Asia as far as Iran. It occurs in the south of England but is absent in Ireland. The species is sometimes fairly abundant in fields of flowering clover, or lucerne; the butterflies stay on flowers overnight. The blue-green caterpillar has dark dorsal and side stripes and red-yellow spots. The pupa is green-brown.

The Chalk-hill Blue chooses habitats similar to those of the above-mentioned species, particularly on chalk and limestone downland. The two species are often found together. It occurs throughout most of Europe, with the exception of Ireland, Scandinavia, Denmark and Portugal. The species is very much sought after by collectors in England; this is why hundreds of different forms have been described and named. As in many other species of this family, there is a marked difference in colouring between the male and the female. The species was originally described from specimens found in Austria (Graz). The blue-green hairy caterpillar has yellow stripes and rows of yellow dots. The pupa is yellowish-brown.

L. bellargus:
V.—VI.,
VII.—VIII.
Caterpillar:
VII., then from autumn to V.
Foodplant:
Horseshoe vetch.

L. coridon:
VI.—VIII.
Egg:
From autumn to IV.
Caterpillar:
IV. to VI.
Foodplant:
Horseshoe vetch.

L. bellargus:
1 — underside of wings (male),
2 — male,
3 — female,
4 — f. *ceronus* (female)
L. coridon:
5 — underside of wings (male),
6 — female,
7 — male

Dingy Skipper

Erynnis tages LINNAEUS, 1758

Hesperiidae

Large Chequered Skipper
Heteropterus morpheus PALLAS, 1771

Chequered Skipper
Carterocephalus palaemon PALLAS, 1771

The Dingy Skipper is widespread throughout Europe and Asia as far as China. It appears in early spring and has only one brood in northern areas, but usually two generations in the south. It inhabits clearings, meadows and hillsides; sometimes it settles together with the Blues on the damp ground to drink. It flies rapidly, low above the ground.

The Large Chequered Skipper lives in the area extending from northern Spain to Siberia and Korea. Although abundant in certain woodland clearings and sheltered woodland valleys, its incidence in central Europe tends to be local.

The distribution range of the Chequered Skipper stretches from western Europe to Japan and North America. In the Alps it is found at altitudes of about 1500 m in wooded areas. The smaller, darker coloured specimens from high mountains are known as f. *freyi* Hellw. It flies very swiftly and low above the ground like most species of this family.

E. tages:
IV.—VIII. one or two generations.
Caterpillar: In VI., then from summer to spring.
Foodplants: Bird's-foot trefoil, eryngium, etc.

H. morpheus:
VI.—VII., sometimes also in VIII.
Caterpillar: From summer to spring.
Foodplants: Purple moor grass, false brome grass.

C. palaemon:
V.—VI., in the mountains also VII.
Caterpillar: From autumn to spring.
Foodplants: Brome grass, false brome and other grasses.

E. tages:
1 — female,
3 — underside of wings (male),
H. morpheus:
2 — underside of wings (male),
4 — male
C. palaemon:
5 — female,
6 — underside of wings (male)

CATCHING OF BUTTERFLIES, CATERPILLARS AND PUPAE

It is rather difficult to say what kind of place is most suitable for catching butterflies and moths. They are found in so many different localities, even in big cities, but naturally the country-side, forests, meadows, fields and mountains are more pleasant places to visit than towns. During this century butterflies everywhere have been getting scarcer, undoubtedly as a result of the increasing pollution of the environment, interference with and destruction of natural vegetation and the excessive use of insecticides in agriculture.

With the exception of the cold winter months, butterflies and moths can be collected almost all the year round. The spring species emerge in the second half of March, and even earlier if it is warm enough, sometimes as early as February. The hibernating species also can be seen already during the first sunny days of spring. In autumn *Lepidoptera* can still be found in November or the beginning of December, particularly moths of the Geometer species. Even in winter one can collect them in caves, cellars, arches, farm buildings and similar places where various moths and butterflies, like the Nymphalids, hibernate. Catching butterflies is most rewarding in the morning because they are then at their most active, provided it is a sunny day. During the late afternoon, and also in cloudy weather, butter-flies tend to fly much less and therefore are more difficult to find.

Individual butterfly species have different habitat require-ments and most collectors are aware of this fact. They also have individual habits of flight, rest and feeding, and even prefer different kinds of flowers. Some species favour putrefying organic matter. The Purple Emperors seek horse dung and the Poplar White Admiral is fond of settling on rubbish heaps near weekend cottages. Most butterflies however are, above all, attracted to flowers which are rich in nectar. The Scarce Swallowtail, for example, likes to visit flowering lilac. Flowering thistles are sought after by Fritillaries and so are the hawkweeds, where they often stay overnight. The Apollo settles almost exclusively on flowering thistles; Satyrids prefer cruciferous plants or members of the Campion family. The Blues and Hesperids prefer the thyme, bramble, rock rose or knapweed.

Hunting Methods

Butterflies are caught by means of an entomological net fastened to a wooden, bamboo, or metal handle. The round collapsible net frame can easily be placed into a rucksack or pocket. Most of the nets used nowadays have a diameter of about 30 cm. Nets with fixed frames, suitable for transportation by car, have become popular in recent years.

The length of the handle or stick is optional. Some collectors prefer handles consisting of several parts that may be shortened or lengthened according to need. The depth of the net is approximately double the diameter of the frame so that it can be folded to prevent the captured butterfly escaping. One has to be careful not to make too vigorous or excessively frequent sweeps of the net because the butterfly inside may easily be injured or its wings damaged.

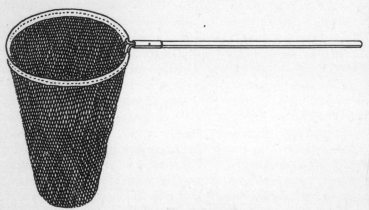

Fig. 4. Butterfly net.

One way of killing the captured butterfly is to carefully compress the thorax from below, taking care to maintain the wings in resting position, i.e. uppersides together. The most robust butterflies and some moths, such as the Hawk-moths, Tiger-moths, etc., or conversely, the smallest ones, may be killed by being allowed to fly into an uncorked killing jar, carefully placed in the net and closed as soon as the butterfly enters it. Similarly the butterflies killed by compression of the thorax may be put into the killing jar for a few minutes to make sure they are dead.

The killing jar is made of glass or plastic and has a wide opening. About a quarter of it is filled with pressed cotton wool soaked in chloroform or ethyl acetate. More experienced collectors use cyanide of potassium. A few crystals are placed on the bottom of the killing jar and encased in plaster of Paris. The insects are killed by vapours of hydrocyanic acid and

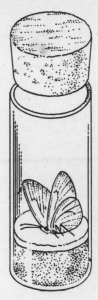

Fig. 5.
Killing jar.

Fig. 6. Butterfly bag.

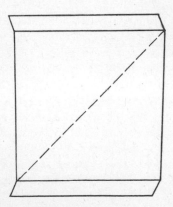

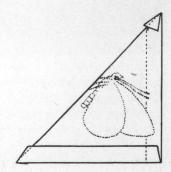

171

ammonia produced in the killing jar. Of course, this agent is very dangerous and in many countries can only be obtained under licence. It is practical to have several killing jars available in order to sort out the captured butterflies. The small delicate specimens are separated from the large ones, the white butterflies are separated from the dark ones, etc. The dead butterfly specimens are kept in small triangular paper envelopes provided with labels where the date and place of finding are recorded. Alternatively it is possible to pin the butterflies on the spot, using the fine long entomological pins and set them in boxes lined with cork. Entomological forceps can be very useful in this case.

Naturally, this short account of some of the principles of collecting butterflies does not exhaust the subject. Many specialized methods are used, particularly in collecting the night-flying moths, e.g. light traps, the use of bait, etc. These methods will not be described in details as we are mainly concerned with butterflies.

Collecting and Breeding of Caterpillars

Captured caterpillars are best kept in tin-plate or plastic boxes of different sizes with a gauze covering. The essential instruments needed are: entomological forceps, a knife, or seccateurs for cutting twigs. The caterpillars should not be overcrowded in the boxes. Hairy and smooth caterpillars should not be kept together. After returning from a collecting excursion the caterpillars should be transferred to larger rearing cages.

Caterpillars are collected either singly or en masse. Mass collection is employed mainly in research, e.g. studies of the composition of the insect fauna on cultural plants, etc. Then, it usually does not matter a great deal if the caterpillars are injured, as often only numerical data about their incidence are wanted. Sometimes collecting may be carried out by the so-called "sweeping" method. Instead of the usual net, a durable coarse linen bag is attached to a firm frame with a handle. The frame may be either round of rectangular. The handle is usually gripped in both hands, as sweeping requires physical effort and may be quite tiring. The opening of the net is swept over the foliage as if in an attempt to scythe off the tops of plants or branches. The caterpillars resting on the plants are shaken off into the bag. It may be difficult to identify the foodplant of the captured caterpillar unless the sweeping was performed in a monoculture area (e.g a sugar-beet field). The method is more suitable for collecting beetles, Plant-bugs, Hymenopterous and some of the Dipterous insects, which are less vulnerable than caterpillars. Caterpillars for breeding may be collected by "beating". Branches of trees or shrubs are beaten with a stick and the caterpillars fall into an inverted open umbrella, a beating tray or an outspread sheet.

The least injurious method of collecting is that of individual hand-picking, searching through leaves, twigs and other places visited by caterpillars.

The rearing cages should have a base measurement of approximately 25 ×25 ×10 cm. A wooden frame, about 40 cm high, is built on the wooden base, to support netting or gauze that forms the roof and sides of the cage. On one side there should be a well-fitting door or a sliding glass panel through which fresh food can be put in and the excrement removed. Caterpillars can also be successfully reared in glass jars, in boxes made of transparent plastic, or in flower-pots. The container should be covered with a piece of cloth or organdie, fixed by an elastic band, and it should be kept in places protected from direct sunshine. Food stays fresh longer in such containers but the excrement must be removed more often to prevent the formation of mould and possible introduction of an infection. Caterpillars in captivity need plenty of food and space. Some species, as for example the Large White, bear collective breeding quite well; others may turn cannibalistic and must be reared separately.

Before pupating, the caterpillars become restless and spend long periods of time — often hours — crawling round the walls of the rearing cage or container. If crowded, they disturb one another and the new soft pupae may be injured. Therefore suitable conditions for pupating should be ensured. The moths, especially Noctuids, often pupate underground, so a layer of soil should be put on the bottom of the rearing box for them. The pupae of butterflies are usually attached to twigs and plants with which they should be supplied in sufficient quantity. Caterpillars may fix themselves to the walls or ceiling of the rearing cage. They must be given the optimal conditions to be able to pupate in peace.

More complicated but, at the same time, more interesting is the breeding of young caterpillars. Experienced collectors breed butterflies directly from the eggs. It is extremely difficult even for experts to find butterfly eggs in nature and quite impossible without a profound knowledge of the habits of individual species. For this reason it is more common to capture the female and get it to lay eggs in captivity. Butterfly females, especially, require enough space for flying and must have the correct food-plants to lay the eggs upon. Some of the moths are more modest in this respect and often lay eggs onto all sorts of surfaces, e.g. paper, carton, cloth, etc. Sometimes, however, even here one may meet with unforeseen difficulties.

Collecting and Breeding of Pupae

Collecting pupae is usually undertaken during bad weather or in the seasons when flying butterflies are scarce, i.e. early spring or autumn. The equipment is similar to that used for collecting caterpillars, with a small spade and rake added. It requires a bit of a knack to find the pupae, as the caterpillars frequently pupate quite far from the place where they have developed. They may be found in the forks of branches, cracks in the bark of trees, garden fences, milestones, stalks of grass, etc. Pupae of many *Lepidoptera*, e.g. the Hawk-moths, Geometer moths, etc. lie underground, either close to the surface or deeper — though never deeper than 30 cm.

The collected pupae are put on a dish with a layer of clean sand and then placed in the rearing cage. Pupae do not demand as much attention as caterpillars but should be sprayed now and then with tepid water. Depending on the temperature, the

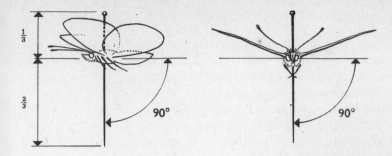

Fig. 7. Correct pinning of a butterfly.

butterflies hatch in several days or up to three weeks during the summer season. Pupae found before the natural time of hibernation must be exposed to cold in refrigeration for several weeks if butterflies are needed out of season, and a period of low temperature is necessary for the phase of their development known as the diapause. Dead pupae are recognized by their immobility and hardened abdominal segments.

Pinning of Butterflies

A butterfly is killed as described above and then a pin is inserted through the centre of its thorax from above and the butterfly is pushed up along the pin to about two thirds of its length. The pins are made of steel, about 36—38 mm long and of various thicknesses. The sizes 0, 1, 2 and 3 are all that are required for the European butterflies. The larger pins 4, 5 and 6 are designed for the more robust exotic butterflies. The thin pins 00 and 000 are used to pin the smaller moths. The smallest 2—3 mm moths are pinned with short sharpened pieces of fine steel wire.

Two types of forceps are used in the setting of butterflies. The butterflies that are to be pinned are handled with soft forceps made of thin steel plate. Harder forceps are used to separate stiffened wings. Some people like to use forceps with curved tips for moving pinned butterflies onto the setting boards or into the collection. Setting needles are also sometimes helpful. However, many collectors do not use them, preferring entomological pins of varying thickness inserted in wooden or glass handles.

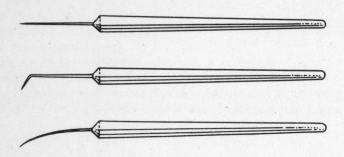

Fig. 8. A — pins
B — different types of entomological forceps.

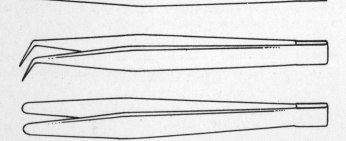

Before adding a butterfly to a collection it should be stretched out on a setting board. This usually consists of two parallel pieces of soft lime or poplar wood, or cork which may be covered in paper, with a groove between them for the butterfly's body. The two panels are attached to a wooden base. The groove is filled with cork or other suitable soft material easy to

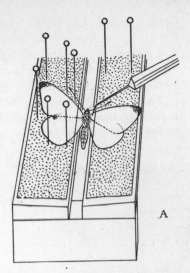

Fig. 9. Set butterflies:
   A — method of setting
   B — traversable setting board with a screw
   C — fixed setting board with butterflies.

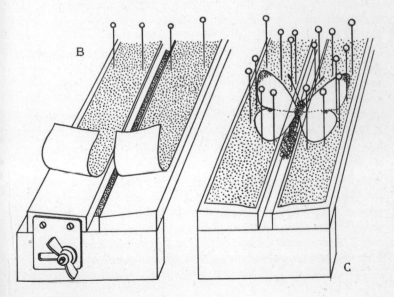

insert pins into. The width of the groove varies from 3 to 8 mm for European *Lepidoptera*. Setting boards with a wider groove, 9 to 12 mm, are used to set the large Hawk-moths, Silkworms, etc. Some exotic species require even wider grooves. The length of the setting board is 30 cm as a rule.

The pin, stuck vertically through the thorax of the specimen, is inserted straight in the middle of the groove so that the basis of the wings is at the level of the edges of the groove. The exact pinning of the specimen through the centre of the thorax and the positioning onto the setting board is essential. Otherwise it would be necessary to insert the pin crookedly in the collection box in order to obtain a horizontal position of the specimen, i.e. the wings parallel with the bottom of the box.

Setting of Wings

With the pinned butterfly properly placed on the setting board you can start setting. A pin may be inserted to the left of the abdomen to prevent the specimen rotating round the ento-mological pin. A band of cellophane or tracing linen is placed across the left pair of wings and fastened by a pin at the top of the setting board. With the assistance of the setting needle the forewing is carefully advanced until its posterior margin and the longitudinal axis of the setting board form a right angle, and it is held in place by light pressure with the cellophane strip. In a similar way the hindwing is brought forward, so that it becomes partially overlapped by the forewing. The wings are levelled by pushing the needle point gently against the strongest anterior veins and so avoid tearing them. Sharp pins with coloured glass heads, usually used by tailors, are most suitable for this work. The same procedure is repeated with the right pair of wings. Several pins are then inserted round the wings through the cellophane, so that they are pressed down to the board and cannot move. The strips of cellophane should be wide enough to cover the whole surface of the wings.

The antennae and abdomen are then moved into natural

positions and the body is supported by a wisp of cotton wool so as not to become distorted during drying.

To start with we set butterflies one by one; later, having gained more experience, we use longer bands of cellophane to cover more specimens at the same time. When the butterfly is completely dry in a matter of ten to fifteen days the wings remain in the fixed position after the pins and cellophane strips are removed.

Dried butterflies, stored in paper envelopes during collecting excursions, must be moistened before setting. Finely sieved sand, boiled to rid it of any mould, is used for this purpose. The excess water is poured away and the moist sand is spread in a dish or tin with a lid. Pinned butterflies are inserted in the sand or the envelopes containing individual specimens are put in. The addition of a chemical agent preventing putrefaction and mould is advisable. The dish is then covered with a sheet of glass. The moistened butterflies are ready to set the following day. Larger specimens may require longer periods of relaxing.

Relaxing of the robust specimens (the Hawk-moths, Silk-worms, exotic species, etc.) may be speeded up by an injection of hot water in the thorax, close to the basis of the wings.

The setting of relaxed specimens is carried out in the same way as with the freshly bred or caught ones, but it is rather more difficult because they do retain a certain degree of stiffness.

Data Labels

As soon as the specimen is taken off the setting board it should be provided with a data label, placed underneath the butterfly, and containing the following information:
1. Locality of capture, altitude, country.
2. Date of capture and the name of the collector.

Further supplementary data are left to the collector's discretion. Details of the habitat are sometimes added in the case some rare species but usually it is not necessary as far as the of butterflies are concerned. The name of the host is entered in the data label of the parasitic insects, and similarly the name of the plant on which the larva of a small moth has been found, may be recorded. It should also be made clear whether the specimen was bred or caught wild. The abbreviations used are: e. o. (ex ovo — from egg), e.l. (ex larva — from caterpillar), e. p. (ex pupa — from pupa). It stands to reason that in this case the name of the place where the specimen was collected is recorded and not the locality where the imago emerged.

Preparation of Caterpillars

The preparation of caterpillars has already been described in many handbooks. The dry prepared specimens of caterpillars, known as "blown larvae", however, are only rarely found in collections nowadays. They are not suited for scientific work as the internal organs are removed and the external characteristics often obliterated. It is only the coloration that is fairly well preserved in dry caterpillars. For reference purposes caterpillars are usually kept in 70% alcohol or special liquid preservatives. To emphasize the morphological features by tightening of the skin, the specimens are boiled before being put into the liquid. The dry specimens may be conveniently included in school collections to demonstrate the course of development of a butterfly or moth species, say, a pest.

If preservation of pupae is desired, all that is necessary is to kill them. Pupae are even rarer in collections than caterpillars. It is more common to keep the empty chrysalis shell left after the emerging of the butterfly and it looks best if left attached to the stem or twig on which it pupated.

Starting a Collection

The extent and arrangement of the collection depends on the intentions and resources of each collector. The set butterflies are placed in boxes provided with a pressed peat, cork, or polystyrene bottom lining, which makes for easy pinning. The polystyrene bottom layer must not come into direct contact with some disinfectants (e.g. paradichlorbenzol) as it may dissolve and become damaged. The boxes are, as a rule, glass-topped so that the insects can most easily be viewed. The boxes should be kept in well-fitting cases as light and dust may otherwise damage the collection.

Collections should be disinfected from time to time to eradicate the insects feeding on the dry specimens, e.g. Museum beetles, mites, book-lice, clothes moths, etc. They may be killed by various chemicals, most commonly paradichlorbenzol or some modern volatile insecticides. Some collectors dust the boxes with DDT or HCH. Insect pests generally attack collections that have been stored for some time without being handled, then they can multiply unnoticed. A small heap of fine powder signifies the presence of the museum beetle living inside the bodies of the specimens. Book-lice devour the pinned butterflies from the outside, starting with the wings.

It is often argued how many specimens of the same species should be included in a collection. There is no hard and fast rule about this. It is up to the collector himself to adjust his collection according to his own concepts. The collection of a specialist will be entirely different from that of a nature lover who is interested in the fauna of a given region. Museums keep large collections of butterflies and moths; without doubt the largest is the extensive collection owned by the British Museum in their Natural History Department. This was considerably enriched by the donation of Lord W. Rothschild's private collection at Tring, Herts, after the Second World War. By merging the two, a huge collection of Lepidoptera was formed, containing several million reference specimens. Specialists from all over the world constantly visit the Natural History Museum to study this unique collection.

The final layout of a collection will be influenced by the aims of the collector. Some may collect small series of specimens of each species, e.g. 3 pairs; others may accumulate large series, trying to follow the variability of the species. There are specialists who confine themselves to a particular group, e.g. the butterflies, Hawk-moths, Whites, etc. A beginner should, at first, attempt to acquire a general knowledge about the fauna of the surrounding environment, only later focusing his attention on a smaller group of lepidopterous insects to study in detail, e.g. from the point of view of the whole of Europe, Palearctic Region or the whole world. There is no need to emphasize that the less attractive butterflies and certain of the moths should not be ignored, especially the small ones, the knowledge of which is lagging behind that of the larger species.

A well kept collection can last for a long time. There is even one made in the 18th century during the reign of Queen Anne housed at Oxford University Museum which is still in excellent condition and used constantly for reference purposes. Even a small collection with precise and reliable data is of scientific and aesthetic value and enriches the collector's knowledge.

BIBLIOGRAPHY

Baynes, E.S.A.: *A Revised Catalogue of Irish Macrolepidoptera.* E. W. Classey, Hampton, Middlesex, 1964.

Beaufoy, S.: *Butterfly Lives.* Collins, London, 1947.

Bergmann, A.: *Die Großschmetterlinge Mitteldeutschlands,* 5 vol. Jena and Leipzig, 1952—55.

Bourgogne, J.: *Ordre des Lépidoptères.* Grassé, Traité de Zoologie, vol. 10, Masson et Cie., Paris, 1950.

Danesch, O. and Dierl, W.: *Schmetterlinge, vol. I. Tagfalter.* Belser Verlag, Stuttgart, 1965.

Döhring, E.: *Zur Morphologie der Schmetterlingseier.* Akademie-Verlag, Berlin, 1955.

Dos Passos, C. F.: *A Synonymic List of the Nearctic Rhopalocera.* The Lepidopterists' Society, Memoir 1. New Haven, 1964.

Ford, E. B.: *Butterflies.* Collins, London, 1946.

Forster, W.: *Biologie der Schmetterlinge.* Franckh'sche Verlagshandlung, Stuttgart, 1954.

Forster, W. and Wohlfart, Th.: *Die Schmetterlinge Mitteleuropas.* Franckh'sche Verlagshandlung, Stuttgart, 1955.

Harz, K. and Wittstadt, H.: *Wanderfalter.* Die Neue Brehm-Bücherei, vol. 191. A. Ziemsen Verlag, Lutherstadt Wittenberg, 1957.

Hemming, F.: *The Generic Names of the Butterflies and their Type-species (Lepidoptera, Rhopalocera).* Bulletin 9. British Museum (Natural History) London, 1967.

Hering, M.: *Biologie der Schmetterlinge.* J. Springer Verlag, Berlin, 1926.

Higgins, L. G. and Rilley, N. D.: *A Field Guide to the Butterflies of Britain and Europe.* Collins, London, 1970.

Higgins, L. G. and Riley, N. D.: *Tagfalter Europas und Nordwestafrikas.* Hamburg and Berlin, 1971.

Johnson, C. G.: *Migration and Dispersal of Insects by Flight.* Methuen & Co. Ltd., London, 1969.

Koch, M.: *Wir bestimmen Schmetterlinge. I. Tagfalter Deutschlands.* Neumann Verlag, Radebeul und Berlin, 1963.
Kostrowicki, A.S.: *Geography of Palearctic Papilionidae.* Panstwowe Wydawnictwo Naukowe, Cracow, 1969.
Kurentzov, A.J.: *The Butterflies of the Far East USSR.* Nauka, Leningrad, 1970.

Langer, T.W.: *Nordens Dagsommefugle i farver.* Munksgaards Forlag A.S., Copenhagen, 1958.
Latouche, Y.: *Schmetterlinge. Europäische Arten.* Delphin Verlag, Stuttgart and Zürich, 1967.

Moucha, J. and Choc, V.: *Taschenatlas der Tagfalter.* Verlag Werner Dausien, Hanau/Main, 1968.
Moucha, J. and Procházka, F.: *Die schönste Tagfalter.* Verlag Werner Dausien, Hanau/Main, 1963.
Munroe, E.: *The Classification of the Papilionidae (Lepidoptera)* The Canadian Entomologist, Suppl. 17. Ottawa, 1960.

Newman, L.H. and Mansell, E.: *The Complete British Butterflies in Colour.* Ebury Press and Michael Joseph, London, 1968.
Niculescu, E.V. and König, F.: *Lepidoptera.* Partea generala, Fauna Republicii Soc. Romania. Bucharest, 1970.

Pagenstecher, A.: *Die geographische Verbreitung der Schmetterlinge.* Fischer Verlag, Jena, 1909.
Peters, W.: *Provisional Check-List of the Butterflies of the Ethiopian Region.* E.W. Classey, Hampton, Middlesex, 1952.
Portier, P.: *Biologie des Lépidoptères.* Paul Lechevalier, Paris, 1949.

Schulte, A.: *Schmetterlinge.* Fackelträger-Verlag Schmidt-Küster, Hannover, 1965.
Seitz, A.: *Die Großschmetterlinge der Erde,* 16. vol. A. Kerner Verlag, Stuttgart, 1906 and later.
Stokoe, W. J.: *The Observer's Book of Butterflies.* Frederick Warne and Co. Ltd., New York, 1969.

Tabuchi, Y.: *The Alpine Butterflies of Japan.* Hobundo, Tokyo, 1959.

Verity, R.: *Le Farfalle Diurne d'Italia.* 5. vol. Marzocco, Florence, 1940—53.

Williams, C. B.: *Die Wanderflüge der Insekten*. Verlag Paul Parey, Hamburg and Berlin, 1961.

Williams, C. B.: *The Migration of Butterflies*. Oliver and Boyd, Edinburgh and London, 1930.

Wolfsberger, J.: *Die Macrolepidopteren-Fauna des Gardaseegebietes*. Memorie Museo Civico Stor. Nat., Verona, 1966.

INDEX OF COMMON NAMES

Admiral, Poplar   82
          Red   112
          Southern White   80
          White   80
Apollo   48
          Clouded   46
Argus, Scotch   150

Blue, Adonis   164
          Chalk-hill   164
Brimstone   72
Brown, Arran   152
          Dusky Meadow   144
          Large Wall   130
          Meadow   142
          Wall   130

Camberwell Beauty   116
Cardinal   106
Comma Butterfly   126
Copper, Large   158
          Purple-edged   160
          Purple-shot   160
          Scarce   158
          Small   162
          Sooty   162
          Violet   162

Dryad   146

Emperor, Lesser Purple   74
          Purple   76

False Comma   120
Festoon, Southern   44
          Spanish   44
Fritillary, Dark Green   98
          Heath   88
          High Brown   100

Fritillary, Lesser Marbled   94
         Lesser Spotted   86
         Marsh   84
         Niobe   102
         Pallas's   108
         Pearl-bordered   92
         Queen of Spain   96
         Silver-washed   104
         Small Pearl-bordered   90
         Spotted   86

Glider, Common   78
      Hungarian   78
Grayling   134
      Great Banded   138
      Woodland   140

Hairstreak, Green   156
        Brown   154
        Purple   154
        White-letter   156
Heath, Chestnut   148
     Pearly   148
     Small   148
Hermit   136

Map Butterfly   110

Orange Tip   60

Painted Lady   114
Peacock Butterfly   122

Ringlet, Large   152
      Woodland   150

Skipper, Chequered   166
      Dingy   166
      Large Chequered   166
Speckled Wood   128
Swallowtail   40
      Scarce   42

Tortoiseshell, Large   118
      Small   124

White, Bath 58
   Black-veined 64
   Dark-veined 56
   Fenton's Wood 62
   Green-veined 54
   Large 50
   Marbled 132
   Small 52
   Wood 62

Yellow, Berger's Clouded 66
   Clouded 70
   Moorland Clouded 68
   Pale Clouded 66

INDEX OF LATIN NAMES

Aglais urticae   124
Anthocharis cardamines   60
Apatura ilia   74
Apatura iris   76
Aporia crataegi   64
Araschnia levana   110
Argynnis paphia   104
Argyronome laodice   108

Brenthis ino   94
Brintesia circe   138

Callophrys rubi   156
Carterocephalus palaemon   166
Chazara briseis   136
Clossiana euphrosyne   92
Clossiana selene   90
Coenonympha arcania   148
Coenonympha glycerion   148
Coenonympha pamphilus   148
Colias australis   66
Colias crocea   70
Colias hyale   66
Colias palaeno   68

Erebia aethiops   150
Erebia euryale   152
Erebia ligea   152
Erebia medusa   150
Erynnis tages   166
Euphydryas aurinia   84

Fabriciana adippe   100
Fabriciana niobe   102

Gonepteryx rhamni   72

Heodes alciphron   160
Heodes tityrus   162

Heodes virgaureae   158
Heteropterus morpheus   166
Hipparchia fagi   140
Hipparchia semele   134
Hyponephele lycaon   144

Inachis io   122
Iphiclides podalirius   42
Issoria lathonia   96

Lasiommata maera   130
Lasiommata megera   130
Leptidea morsei   62
Leptidea sinapis   62
Limenitis camilla   80
Limenitis populi   82
Limenitis reducta   80
Lycaena dispar   158
Lycaena helle   162
Lycaena phlaeas   162
Lysandra bellargus   164
Lysandra coridon   164

Maniola jurtina   142
Melanargia galathea   132
Melitaea didyma   86
Melitaea trivia   86
Mellicta athalia   88
Mesoacidalia aglaja   98
Minois dryas   146

Neptis rivularis   78
Neptis sappho   78
Nymphalis antiopa   116
Nymphalis polychloros   118
Nymphalis vau-album   120

Palaeochrysophanus hippothoë   160
Pandoriana pandora   106
Papilio machaon   40
Pararge aegeria   128
Parnassius apollo   48
Parnassius mnemosyne   46
Polygonia c-album   126
Pieris brassicae   50
Pieris bryoniae   56